SPOKEN

INTO

BEING

SPOKEN INTO BEING

DIVINE ENCOUNTERS THROUGH STORY

— MICHAEL E. WILLIAMS —

UPPER ROOM BOOKS®
NASHVILLE

Upper Room Books® website: books.upperroom.org

Upper Room®, Upper Room Books®, and design logos are trade-
marks owned by The Upper Room®, Nashville, Tennessee. All
rights reserved.

Scripture quotations not otherwise marked are from the New
Revised Standard Version Bible, copyright 1989 National Coun-
cil of the Churches of Christ in the United States of America.
Used by permission. All rights reserved.

Scripture quotations marked KJV are taken from the King James
Version of the Bible.

Cover design: Charles Brock | Faceout Studio
Cover image: Javier Pardina | Stocksy
Interior design and typesetting: PerfecType | Nashville, TN

Library of Congress Cataloging-in-Publication Data
Names: Williams, Michael E. (Michael Edward), 1950– author.
Title: Spoken into being : divine encounters through story /
  Michael E. Williams.
Description: Nashville : Upper Room Books, 2017. |
Identifiers: LCCN 2016056671 (print) | LCCN 2017020550
  (ebook) | ISBN 9780835817080 (Mobi) | ISBN 9780835817097
  (Epub) | ISBN 9780835817073 (print)
Subjects: LCSH: Storytelling—Religious aspects—Christianity.
Classification: LCC BT83.78 (ebook) | LCC BT83.78 .W63 2017
  (print) | DDC 231.7—dc23
LC record available at https://lccn.loc.gov/2016056671

For
MINERVA CHERRY CHAMBERS,
my great-aunt,
who first told me stories
and
FREDA CHERRY WILLIAMS,
my mother,
who kept that tradition alive
in our family

CONTENTS

ACKNOWLEDGMENTS

I am grateful to have grown up in a family graced by storytellers. My "Aintie" Minerva Cherry Chambers, my great-aunt on my mother's side, was the first teller of stories in my life, though she would have been offended to be called a storyteller. To her, the word *storyteller* meant "liar." She is my matron saint of narrative.

I am fortunate that my mother, Freda Cherry Williams, continued the tradition of keeping her family stories alive by retelling Aintie's stories as well as others. Her ongoing practice of our family tradition cemented the stories in my imagination.

I am indebted to Barbara McDermitt, one of my professors in the 1970s at Northwestern University, who first said to me, "You know that you're a storyteller, don't you?" I hadn't realized that about myself until that day. In 1979, I returned to Tennessee after attending school in the Chicago area and made my first visit to the National Storytelling Festival. The friends I made there over the years became my mentors in the art of telling stories. I am thankful for their continued influence in my life.

I am grateful to Rita Collett for suggesting that I might have a book in me that Upper Room Books would be interested in publishing. Also, my heartfelt thanks go to Joanna Bradley, my patient and faithful editor, who "got" what

I was attempting to do and, through her insightful comments and suggestions, made this a far better book in its maturity than it was when it began its life.

Finally, I offer thanks to the many people who have been participants in storytelling workshops I have led over the years. We are partners in keeping this ancient art alive.

TELL ME A STORY

[A]

Long ago, in Kentucky, I, a boy, stood
By a dirt road, in the first dark, and heard
The great geese hoot northward.

I could not see them, there being no moon
And the stars sparse.   I heard them.

I did not know what was happening in my heart.

It was the season before the elderberry blooms,
Therefore they were going north.

The sound was passing northward.

[B]

Tell me a story.

In this century, and moment, of mania,
Tell me a story.

Make it a story of great distances, and starlight.

11

The name of the story will be Time,
But you must not pronounce its name.

Tell me a story of deep delight.*

*Robert Penn Warren, "Tell Me a Story," *Audubon: A Vision* (New York: Random House, Inc., 1969), 31–32.

PREFACE

Everyone is a storyteller. I didn't say that everyone *could be* a storyteller; everyone already *is* a storyteller, whether he or she realizes and acknowledges it or not. After forty years of telling stories and helping other people tell stories, I have learned this fact. From the first time a baby grunts and reaches for a cookie before he has finished his pureed green beans, he has begun to tell a story (albeit nonverbally) of choice and desire. When a parent asks a child what happened today at school and refuses to take "Nuthin!" for an answer, the child begins to frame her experience as a narrative. The astute parent knows that persistently asking the question, "Then what happened?" helps drive the sequence of events that become the story of the day. Stories arise at bedtime when a parent or grandparent opens a book and reads aloud or turns off the light and creates a world of historical or completely imaginary characters and events, a world in which both teller and listener take part until one or the other falls asleep. Stories erupt around the dinner table with the words, "You won't believe what happened at work today." Or they emerge slowly, accompanied by, "Did I ever tell you about the time . . . ?"

Human beings live in story like fish live in water. We literally experience our lives as a narrative—not as a series of random events but as a sequence of connected occasions and experiences stitched together in narrative form. In this way, our experiences take on coherence and meaning. We learn to understand the world, other people, and God through a narrative lens. We also live surrounded by God like the very air we breathe, often invisible to us but absolutely necessary for life. This is why Paul can say to those gathered at the Temple of Athena that God is the one in which we live and move and have our being. (See Acts 17:28.) For this reason, when we speak of our experiences of God, we most often tell stories. Telling stories is not only a way of framing our understanding of the world and the people around us but also the means by which we speak of our divine encounters as well.

During the past fifty years, the art of storytelling has received renewed interest and appreciation. Storytelling festivals have sprung up all over the world, and with them, a class of performer known as the "professional storyteller" has emerged. Professional storytellers make their living traveling and telling stories in schools, theaters, churches, and other venues. Most of these performers are quite gifted, work hard at their craft, and deserve the attention and fees they receive. But I have noticed an unintended shadow side to the emergence of the "professional storyteller."

Throughout history, storytelling has been a popular art, something practiced by a wide variety of people in numerous and various settings. Of course some, because of their gifts, became associated with the artful telling of stories, but this identification didn't mean that the craft of storytelling belonged to the professional. The shadow of the professionalization of storytelling is revealed when people who otherwise might offer stories to their class at school, to their congregation at church, or to their children or grandchildren at home, choose not to. They say, "Since I can't tell a story like (insert name of professional storyteller), I won't tell one at all." Let me be clear: The people who make their living by telling stories do not intend to discourage others from doing so. In fact, the storytellers I know want their listeners to discover and tell their own stories. Even so, a storyteller's best efforts at encouraging others can have the unintended opposite effect.

The first thing we need to do is reclaim storytelling as an art form for amateurs. People who love stories can be taught to tell them. Their audience may be two youngsters who are fighting sleep with all their might or a classroom of second graders or a family gathered around a table during the holidays. The size of the audience is not what makes the storyteller!

The first book I had published, *Friends for Life*, consisted of fifty-two stories that could be used in worship. A short time after its publication, I met with a colleague who was the editor of denominational resources. He told me that he had read the book, which pleased me, but then he added that he was disappointed in it. When I asked him to explain, he said, "I knew you had been telling stories for a while and were supposed to be pretty good at it. As I read your book, though, I kept thinking this doesn't seem so hard. Even I could do this." All I could say to him in response was, "Did you ever consider that I intended for you to think exactly that?"

So if after reading *Spoken into Being*, readers go away with the impression that I am especially gifted or an exceptionally accomplished storyteller, then I have failed to convince them that anyone can be a storyteller. But if readers say, "That's not so hard; I can do that," then, in some large measure, I will feel that this book has accomplished its intended task. I hope to help readers recognize the gifts they already possess for telling stories and to encourage them to use those gifts. Maybe they'll even pick up skills in the craft of storytelling along the way.

This book includes retellings of the first two Creation stories in Genesis. Like an overture played before a musical play, the first Creation story provides themes that will be discussed later and will set a tone for the rest of the book. One important reason that I believe all human beings have the capability to be storytellers is because each of us is stamped with the image of God, who spoke the entire universe into being as a story. God's story of Creation sets the standard for all stories that have ever been told and will ever be told. The places, people, and objects that make up every story we tell were present in that first story of Creation. My retelling of the second Creation story, which lies between chapters 2 and 3, will serve as an interlude to set the tone for the latter portion of the book.

In this book, I will take readers on a journey through a series of experiences from my own life. In part, I tell these stories to remind us of our shared experiences, but these stories also introduce me to the readers. Most importantly, however, I hope these stories will serve as an invitation for readers to tell their own stories, using the storytelling prompts at the end of each section. Together, we will discover our sacred stories and the settings, people, and objects that reveal their sacredness to us. We will ask ourselves, *Where are my sacred places? Who has helped me experience God? What holy relics hold importance in my life?* The storytelling prompts are designed to allow the reader to tell his or her own stories in response to the stories I tell.

Stories from scripture and from our own life experiences can be framed in many ways. The two Creation stories at the beginning of Genesis explain in different—some would say contradictory—ways how the universe and human beings came to be. Upon first glance, these two stories offer divergent conclusions about the state of the world and humanity. We frequently find ourselves in such a paradox, living between two different stories that express disparate truths about our world and how we are to understand it. The tension elicited by these seemingly contradictory stories forms the creative environment from which other stories emerge—stories that take us beyond the paradox created by the original narratives.

Sometimes this tension emerges when stories of fear collide with stories of fantasy. When we err on the side of fear, we find ourselves feeling trapped in a single narrative from which we cannot escape and for which we cannot imagine a good ending. When we err on the side of fantasy, we attempt to create an idealized future, a utopian dream that can never be realized fully. When we can embrace the tension that lies between fear and fantasy, holding the two together and refusing to collapse our life story in one direction or the other, we allow for a creative integration of the two that moves us beyond immobilizing, anxiety-producing fear and unrealizable flights of fantasy. When we make the trek beyond fear and fantasy, we move toward the realm of faith. Stories from scripture provide a guide for navigating the extremes of fear and fantasy and lead us toward the mysterious territory of faith. To that effect, later chapters will explore the Joseph saga from Genesis 37–50 and one of Jesus' better known parables, mining both narratives for examples of how we can move beyond stories of fear and fantasy and toward divine encounters fueled by stories of faith.

We can't avoid being formed by stories. Narrative is so all-encompassing that rarely are we consciously aware we are surrounded by it. According to the first Creation story in Genesis, the entire universe is a story being told by God. The stories that capture our attention form us into the persons we are now and shape who we will become in the future. But first, we must ask ourselves, *Which stories will we allow to shape our lives? Will our stories encompass "great distances, and starlight"? Will they be stories of "deep delight," as Robert Penn Warren's poem suggests? Will we live our lives built on a narrative of faith and restoration?* Come on the journey with me, and let's answer these questions together.

Storytelling Prompts

1. Who, if anyone, told you stories when you were young? Did he or she create the stories, offer stories from his or her own life, or tell folk or fairy tales? Who, if anyone, read to you when you were young? What do you recall about that experience? How did you feel toward the teller? If you can remember the stories, share them with others.

2. With whom do you share your own stories—with your children or grandchildren, with your Sunday school class or small group, with friends and family around the dinner table? How does it feel to be the teller of a story? How do you feel toward those who listen? What prompts you to tell stories?

OVERTURE: THE FIRST CREATION STORY

Before anything that ever was
there was nothing, only God breathing into the dark.
It was the deepest darkness ever known
before or since.
The quiet was the most profound silence that ever was
before or since.
In all that darkness and silence, God was lonely.
So God began to spin a web of words carried on God's
    breath.

God said once upon a time there was light.
As the phosphorescent words rolled out of God's mouth,
    there was light.
There wasn't anything to see yet,
but when God saw the light standing next to the darkness
and the darkness standing next to the light,
God said, "This is great."

But God thought there had to be more to this story
since every story needs a place to take place in.
So God said once upon a time there was a large clear bowl
right in the middle of the light and the darkness,
and there were waters above the bowl
and there were waters beneath the bowl

and there were waves above the bowl
and there were waves beneath the bowl.
God said the waters above the bowl we shall call sky
and the waters beneath the bowl we shall call sea
and the waves above the bowl we shall call clouds
and the waves beneath the bowl we shall call . . . waves.

Then God spoke forth a stage upon which this story could
    be enacted.
Let there be dry land, God said,
and sure enough the dry land began to emerge
from the waters of the deep.
On the dry land grew grasses and shrubs and trees.
Now that God had the stage on which the story
of the beginning of all that is would be played out,
there was still something missing.

God said there needs to be characters to act out this story,
so God said once upon a time there was a character
who travels across the sky during the day
and another who travels across the sky during the night
and just so that character who travels at night
doesn't get too lonely and afraid
I will give it thousands of companions.
And the character that travels around during the day God
    called sun.
And the character that travels around during the night
    God called moon
and the nighttime companions to moon God called stars.
And God looked at the great circle dance of the sun and
    moon and stars,
and God said, "This is great."

Then God said once upon a time there were creatures of
    the water.
And sure enough, as soon as God spoke,
the waters were filled with minnows and marlin;
there were bass and catfish in the rivers and creeks and
    seas.
And God said once upon a time there were creatures of
    the air,
and the sky was aflutter with the wings of robins and
    wrens, eagles and condors.
Then God said once upon a time there were four-legged
    creatures,
and you could hear the mooing of the cattle,
the barking of the dogs, and the mewling of the cats.
And once upon a time there were six-legged creatures,
and you could hear the creaking of the crickets,
accompanied by the buzzing of bees and the clicking of
    beetles.
God said once upon a time there were eight-legged
    creatures
and you could almost feel them crawling up your legs!
When God heard the sounds of all the creatures
playing the grand overture of creation God said, "This is
    great."
But there still had to be something more.
I would like someone just like me only a little different,
God said, just different enough to be interesting.

That's when God decided to make human beings.
God said once upon a time there were creatures in the
    divine image
able to tell stories and create worlds and invite others into
    those worlds.

And there were creatures just like God, only a little
     different,
different enough to be very interesting to God and one
     another.
That was when God said, "This must be the greatest story
     ever told!"
They took that for a movie title later, but God said it first.
And when this great story was done, it had taken six days
     to tell.
God was having so much fun that the time had flown by,
but God was tired so on the seventh day God rested
and said to the humans it's time for you to tell the story
     now.
And sure enough from that time to this, across the globe,
women and men around the world have set aside a day
in which the people gather and tell stories, saying,
before the beginning of the beginning of anything that
     ever was
there was God, they say,
and every time that happens somewhere in this great,
     many-storied universe
God says, "This is great!"

CHAPTER 1

What Are Stories, and What Do They Do?

I grew up in a family whose members talked in stories. My earliest memories are set on a porch swing, sitting next to my great-aunt as she tells stories and sings songs to me. Some of these stories, for example those about my great-grandfather, George Washington Cherry, were threads woven into the fabric of my family history. Others recounted the history of the region where we lived, and those stories came to define my sense of place and home. Still others were remnants of ballads that had been brought over from the British Isles, containing echoes of still more ancient narratives. My family members didn't just tell stories; stories were the way they talked.

My mother helped keep our family stories alive for me as a child, even as she added her own. Sometimes she told stories that she hoped would teach me valuable lessons. One was about a man who was so lazy that his neighbors made a plan to scare him into working. They put him on

a wagon and were threatening to run him out of town if
he didn't work harder. They had arranged for one of their
number to offer him a young cow to raise. If he raised the
calf, he would no longer be "trifling" and could remain in
the community. "Well," the man told them, "If I raise that
heifer, I'm going to have to raise a corn crop to feed it. You
know, that's a lot of work."

Another neighbor spoke up, saying, "I'll give you a
wagonload of corn."

The lazy man thought for a minute, then asked, "Is the
corn shelled?"

"Why, no, it ain't shelled," the neighbor responded.
"You want me to shell it for you too?"

The lazy man replied, "Well, if the corn ain't shelled,
you can just drive on with me."

Anytime I didn't want to take out the trash or clean up
after myself or complete any other task my mother asked
me to perform, she would simply say, "Well, if the corn ain't
shelled, you can just drive on with him," and I knew immediately what she meant. Even when my mother corrected
my behavior, she did so through story.

I surrounded myself with stories as well—not only those
told by my family members but also stories from books. I
developed a passion for reading early in life. Though neither of my parents had much formal schooling, both val-
ued education and encouraged my delight in books. They
read to me until I learned to read myself, and they allowed
me to use some of our very limited income to buy books
that struck my fancy. I mostly purchased storybooks, but
I also enjoyed poetry books for children, to which I credit
my lifelong love for the sounds of words and the music that
words make when they are placed in a pleasing order. Many
of the poems contained in these books told stories as well.

I received a few worn-out textbooks that were passed along to me by other family members. Some of these books included a number of Greek and Roman myths and works of literature from the late nineteenth and early twentieth centuries, such as those by Rudyard Kipling and the stories of Doctor Dolittle. I grew to love the stories of other times and cultures and to recognize the ways that they could enrich the life of someone like me—a boy born in the rural South of the United States in the middle of the twentieth century.

Then there was the Bible. My family attended church on a fairly regular basis throughout my childhood. I remember the flannel board that stood in the Sunday school room and the figures that my teacher placed on it to tell stories from scripture. At home, my family stories began to remind me of the stories I heard in church, and my family stories became interlaced with the stories from Sunday school in my mind. The ancient stories from the Jewish and Christian traditions took their place within the same repository of my memory that preserved the oral traditions of my family and the stories I learned from other books.

I don't remember any of my family members telling me Bible stories. I think they must have assumed that to be the responsibility of preachers and Sunday school teachers. They did read the Bible aloud, however, especially stories they thought would be appropriate for a young child like me—stories of lost lambs and coins and the story of David and Goliath. At Christmas, we read the birth narrative of Jesus in the Gospels of Matthew and Luke from the King James Bible. One Bible story that certainly wasn't read or told at home when I was young was that of Jesus' crucifixion. I'm sure my parents thought it would be too violent and might frighten me. One day, I came home from church and announced to my mother, "Did you know that they tried to kill Jesus?"

"Where did you hear that?" my mother inquired.

"I heard the preacher talking about it in church," I told her.

"Well, what do you think about it?" my mother asked.

"Some people tried to kill Jesus, but he sure fooled them, didn't he?" I replied. I'm not sure why that particular story captured my attention. Whatever the reason, I must have been listening to the preacher tell the story in a sermon, and, to tell the truth, my theology of Jesus' passion hasn't progressed much beyond that childhood insight. This childlike understanding still makes sense to me as an adult.

Not everyone is fortunate enough to grow up with family members who talk in stories or appreciate books or even attend church and read the Bible. But everyone can grow in his or her appreciation of stories and use them as companions on his or her spiritual journey.

Stories as Networks of Relationships

Storytelling, along with music, dance, and drama, is one of the most ancient arts that human beings practice in community. Most of the earliest stories we know about were told or sung or danced or enacted, perhaps even using some combination of all four. Stories allow us to tell others what happened in our lives while we were apart or before they were born, thus passing along our own history and the history of where we live. Stories let us express our feelings in all their depth and our thoughts in their complexity. In short, stories help make us human.

Stories are not simply spoken words or documents or recordings. At a fundamental level, stories create a network of relationships. First, a story creates a relationship between the teller or writer and those who will hear, read, or view the story. Anyone who has heard an excellent storyteller perform can attest to the rapport and intimacy between the teller and listeners. A story told aloud benefits from the physical presence of the teller, creating an immediacy and a closeness, but a similar relationship can be built over long distances by anyone who stamps his or her creative work with an effective personal vision. Strangers often approach storytellers or writers and speak to them as if they know each other because they have heard them tell their stories or have read their books or have seen their films.

Second, a story creates a relationship between the teller and listeners and the characters who populate the world of the story. My favorite novel of all time is *To Kill a Mockingbird*. Ever since I first encountered Scout, Jem, Boo, Atticus, and the other citizens of Macomb, Alabama, when I was a teenager, they have lived inside me. In fact, I wanted to grow up to be Atticus Finch. No, I didn't want to practice law; instead, I wanted to be the kind of man the fictional character Atticus embodied. Many of the biblical characters I first heard about as a child in Sunday school are more familiar to me than the people with whom I attended elementary school, though I got to know all of them at roughly the same time in my life. Those characters left an indelible mark on me that has remained to this day.

Third, stories help us relate our outer world of daily experience to the inner world we often call *imagination* or *spirit* or *faith*. Too often the imagination gets a bad reputation. We say "It's just your imagination!" as a way to dismiss an idea as unimportant and disconnected with reality. But without a healthy imagination, we could not participate in biblical stories or any other narratives, nor would we be able to imagine the world being other than it is. If we cannot imagine a better world, we have neither the vision nor the motivation to work toward it. Many cultures recognize that our inner world—our soul or spirit—actually shapes the way we perceive the "real world" because it provides the lens through which we experience "reality."

Right out of college, I was hired by a school system in a small, mostly rural county as a substitute teacher. I spent most of my days taking the place of teachers at the local junior high school. In one instance, I was scheduled to substitute for a week for a teacher who was away for continuing education. Though I always looked over the teacher's lesson plans to acquaint myself with the curriculum, I also asked the students in each class what they had been doing. In this particular class, I asked the question and was met with silence. I rephrased my question by saying, "You were doing something last Friday in class. Can you remember what it was?" Finally, after several unsuccessful attempts to elicit even the slightest response from the class members, a student sitting in the back of the room said, "You don't understand. We're the dumb group. We don't do anything."

Confused and disappointed by this response, I found a portion of *The Odyssey* by Homer in the students' textbook, and that week, the "dumb group" and I studied it. The students loved the part of the story that begins with Odysseus telling the Cyclops, Polyphemus, that his name is Nobody. Later, Odysseus puts out the giant's one eye, causing him to cry out in pain. When the other Cyclopes ask who is hurting him, Polyphemus tells them, "Nobody is hurting me." Later, Odysseus escapes the clutches of the

Cyclops by slipping out of the cave and crawling under the belly of a sheep, so the giant can only feel the wool on the sheep's back rather than the man hiding under its belly.

If children are told stories about themselves that consistently place them in the "dumb group," they will come to believe that characterization of themselves and act out of that narrative. Their outer behavior and expectations are shaped by the stories they carry inside them. But if they hear stories about facing scary monsters and escaping them using their wits and ingenuity, they may just get the idea that they are smarter and more capable than they imagined. The stories that shape our inner world shape our lives as well.

Fourth, the stories that leave a lasting impression on our lives do so because they relate us to that dimension of life we call the *Holy*, the *Sacred*, the *Divine*, or what we as Christians name *God*. These don't have to be overtly religious stories or come from the Bible or another holy book, although those are good places to start. Stories hold mystery and meaning together, and, therefore, they hold the power to put us in touch with the Divine, perhaps even removing the negative stories we have heard about ourselves and replacing them with stories of hope and courage. They help us move beyond our fears and fantasies and remind us of the presence of the Divine within and around us.

One hundred years ago, Rudolf Otto published a book titled *The Idea of the Holy.* In it, he describes the heart of our divine encounters—that which can be experienced but not adequately explained. He has a word for these encounters: the *numinous*. We may point to the numinous with poems, music, stories, or dance, but we can never reduce it to a simple meaning or moral. In other words, the numinous ultimately defies definition. Otto employs the Latin phrase *mysterium tremendum et facinans* to describe the

mystery that overwhelms us, making us tremble and fasci-
nating us at the same time.

When Moses first turns aside to look at the bush that is
burning but not consumed by the flames, we imagine that
his initial motivation is simple curiosity. Soon, however, he
hears a voice coming from the bush and is drawn into a
conversation that will change not only his life but also the
lives of thousands of Hebrew slaves and Egyptian masters,
including Pharaoh. This is certainly an experience of the
numinous since Moses is terrified by the encounter and the
prospect of returning to Egypt. Even so, for all his excuses,
he cannot walk away from the conversation. When Moses
asks for the name of God who is sending him, he is told, "I
AM WHO I AM" (Exod. 3:14) or "I will be who I will be" or
however one translates the four Hebrew letters that are des-
tined to be the name of God for the descendants of those
Hebrew slaves. Those four letters also serve as a testimony
to God's freedom and power; when we encounter the Holy,
we cannot predict who God will be or what God will do.
We cannot confine, define, or explain fully the trajectory of
the Divine. All we can do is to point toward it through the
stories of our encounter with its presence.

What All Stories Have in Common

An almost infinite number of stories exist in the world, as
numerous as all the people who have ever lived. Whether we
are listening to a friend describe his or her recent vacation,
reading a new book, sitting in a darkened movie theater
and enjoying a film, or watching an episode of our favorite
weekly drama or sitcom, we are encountering stories. One
may be a love story and another a story of mystery; one may

make us laugh and another leave us afraid to turn out the light when we go to bed. But all stories share some common characteristics.

All stories create a world and invite the listener, reader, or viewer into that world. The ancient Hebrew storytellers from whom we receive the Creation narratives knew how worlds come into being: They are spoken into being. When God says the word *light*, there is light. When God says the words *land* and *sun* and *moon* and *stars* and *plants* and *creatures* and *human beings*, each appears on the scene. As the storyteller speaks the words of a story, we listeners see those places, characters, and objects in our mind's eye. Instead of saying, "Let there be . . . ," God just as easily could have said, "Once upon a time. . . ."

Stories create new worlds, but they also reveal the nature of the world around us and our place in it. In fact, this is perhaps what stories do best: They tell us who we are in relation to nature, other people, and God. Again and again in that first Creation story, God sees that everything brought into being is either *good* or *very good*. Then, as the story comes to its conclusion, God calls forth creatures who are in "[God's] image, according to [God's] likeness" (Gen. 1:26)—a woman and man who can participate in the ongoing creation by continuing God's storytelling. Humans can tell stories that create worlds and invite others into them, except our worlds are created in the minds and imagination of our listeners. Still, when we tell stories, we experience a deep awareness of the *imago dei*, the divine image that God placed in us from the beginning.

In the process of speaking worlds into being, other elements come into play. If I sound a lot like a teacher of a tenth grade literature class, there is a good reason for that. Every television show, every movie, and every book of fiction or creative nonfiction shares the following similarities: (1) they take place somewhere and sometime, (2) they include a cast of characters, and (3) they include certain objects that help create the place in which the characters live.

Place and Time

Though I spent most of my childhood and youth in Tennessee, my mother, my father, and I moved to Arizona when I was six years old. For three years, we lived in the desert landscape of Sierra Vista near Fort Huachuca in the southernmost part of the state where my father worked as a mechanic. The only vacations I ever remember our family taking involved visiting family back home in Tennessee.

My most vivid memory about those cross-country trips before the days of interstates was that they seemed to last forever. My dad drove a 1953 Chevrolet pickup, and my parents and I did most of our traveling at night because the truck had no air-conditioning. We traveled across New Mexico, Texas, Arkansas, and into Tennessee. As we traveled through the growing darkness each evening, lights began to illuminate the rooms in the houses we passed. I would see families sitting down to eat or lounging on couches, the silver light of the television illuminating their faces. I began to tell myself stories about what they were eating and talking about around the table and the programs they might be watching on television. Sometimes people walked out of the lit rooms and into other rooms where I couldn't see them. I wondered if they were going to read a book, do homework, retrieve a present for a family member, or simply go to bed.

Even as a child, I understood that each of those brightly illuminated rooms contained stories. People lived their lives in those spaces, and anywhere people ate and talked and slept would be filled with the stories of their lives. Rooms in the homes where I grew up and in the homes of relatives where I visited, classrooms and playgrounds of schools I attended, the places I have lived as an adult, the places I attended camp or went on vacation—all are repositories of stories. Even parks I have visited, beaches I have played on, hills and mountains I have hiked, trees under which I have sat—stories reside in those places too.

The time of a story can be very general or quite specific. We all know stories that begin "Once upon a time . . ." or "At the stroke of midnight . . . ." The time is appropriate to the individual story. For example, I could see into the windows of the homes I was passing in my father's truck at dusk, when darkness was expanding and the homes were lit from within. The time of day allowed me to see into the lives of others, all lit up like actors on a stage. Of course, that was never the case during the daylight hours.

In Bible stories, time may be described generally with "In the beginning . . ." or very specifically with "At the sixth hour . . . ." Biblical narratives share this quality with other stories. They can be set in a time frame that is general or specific depending on the requirements of the particular story. Some times of day, such as dawn and dusk, may lend themselves more readily to sharpening our awareness of God's presence. But as the first Creation story reminds us, all time is holy because God's voice set it in motion.

What Makes a Place and Time Sacred?

In the first Creation story, God sees every aspect that the divine voice has called into being and proclaims it good. Therefore, every place in the universe can be considered sacred because it is part of God's story. If every place holds the potential of being recognized as sacred, why do we consider some more sacred than others? Celtic Christians believed that some locations on earth are "thin places," sites where we are more likely to experience the sacred than others. Often, places that we consider sacred have some life-changing story associated with them. I don't mean to imply that the story makes a place sacred; rather, in God's holy narrative that we call the universe, such stories help us recognize the Divine breaking into our lives.

For example, in the book of Genesis, Jacob runs away from his home after conspiring with his mother to trick his blind father into conferring upon him the blessing that belonged to his brother, Esau. While on the run, Jacob camps out under the night sky with only a rock for a pillow—a highly unusual experience for someone who before had preferred staying inside a tent with his mother. Jacob dreams of a ladder populated by angels, and they climb up and down between heaven and earth, resembling shoppers on a mall escalator during the Christmas rush. When Jacob wakes, he recognizes that the story he has experienced in his dream has transformed that place. He exclaims, "Surely the LORD is in this place—and I did not know it!" (Gen. 28:16).

Later, as Jacob prepares to meet his brother, Esau, after many years apart, he fears that his brother is coming with an army to kill him. As Jacob and his wives and children camp by the Jabbok River, Jacob encounters a stranger with whom he wrestles all night. When the stranger demands that Jacob let him go before the sun rises, Jacob (ever ready to take advantage of a situation) exacts a blessing from the stranger as well. Jacob receives a new name: *Israel*. But this time, Jacob does not get away unscathed. No, Jacob limps away with a hip injury sustained during the wrestling match and with his new name, which means "I have wrestled with God and lived to tell the tale." This particular encounter with the Divine transforms both Jacob's physical being and his understanding of who he is.

In both instances, Jacob realizes that a divine encounter has taken place, and the stories of those encounters allow him (and us) to recognize the sacredness of each site. Not every encounter with God is as dramatic as Jacob's, however. When the prophet Elijah expects to encounter God in the wind, in an earthquake, and in a fire, none of those sensational experiences contains God's presence. Rather, God is present in the "still small voice" (1 Kings 19:12, KJV) or, as the New Revised Standard Version translates it, "a sound of sheer silence."

Whether dramatic and sensational or still and small, stories that allow us to recognize sacred places do so by alerting us to God's presence in the here and now. Once we understand that God can enter our lives in any place and at any time, we become aware of the Divine in the present moment.

What, then, makes us aware of certain times that hold the potential for sacred encounters? The first Genesis Creation story takes place *in illo tempore*, that time before time—"Before anything that ever was . . . ." Time begins when God first speaks—not the time that will be determined by the movements of the sun and moon and clocks but the flow of experience called *kairos* (God's time) that intersects with *kronos*, or chronological time (our time).

Sacred time appears whenever we recognize the presence of God's time in the midst of counting our hours, days, months, and years. Still, our own finite narrative, which can be counted and measured, points toward the time that is beyond measure: God's time, eternity.

Characters

The characters who inhabit the world of the any story play a significant role in our experience of the story. In effect, they become our guides, and our attention is directed to various aspects of the story world through their consciousness. In other words, we see the story through their eyes or looking over their shoulders. They will point us toward what is important from their perspective, and we will take in the sights, sounds, and smells of their world. Therefore, the character we choose to lead us through the story will determine much of what we experience there. Take, for example, the story of Joseph in Potiphar's house. If we view the story through Joseph's eyes, we take on the perspective of a slave who, because of his gifts and integrity (and because God is with him), has risen to the rank of chief slave in his master's house. Potiphar entrusts practically everything he owns to Joseph, but Joseph is accused of violating Potiphar's trust by violating his wife. As readers, we know that the accusations against Joseph are untrue, and we can empathize with Joseph. Perhaps we too have been accused of something we didn't do by someone, as in Joseph's case, in a more powerful position than our own. We may ask ourselves how we would have responded in Joseph's position, but this is a question we raise only if we are experiencing the story from Joseph's perspective.

We also can look at the story through Potiphar's wife's eyes. She is not portrayed as a sympathetic character, and the poor soul is not even given a name. We know her exclusively through her relationship to her husband. If we catch a glimpse of the situation through her eyes, we discover a young woman with needs, a young woman whose husband is away on business for Pharaoh. Potiphar leaves his household in the care of Joseph, a young and handsome Hebrew slave. Potiphar's wife's desire for Joseph grows over time and is intensified by his refusal of her advances. Finally, feeling rejected, she accuses him of sexual assault, knowing that she will have the upper hand because she is married to a powerful person.

Perhaps we too have wanted something so badly that we would do almost anything to attain it. But most of us would immediately reject the idea that we could ever want anything so badly as to do what Potiphar's wife did. I'm not just talking about sexual desire, though. What if we wanted a job, a raise, or a promotion so badly that we considered lying about our experience or achievements to get it? What if our child needed medicine or food? What would we be willing to do to get it? Viewing the story over the shoulder of Potiphar's wife raises some questions for us that we may not want to explore—questions that reveal our similarities. She is a person who acts out of her brokenness, just as we are people who act out of our brokenness.

What happens when we look at the story through Potiphar's eyes? He has two people, both of whom he trusts, providing exact opposite versions of the same story. His wife tells him that the Hebrew slave he brought into the house sexually assaulted her. Joseph says that he rebuffed the sexual advances of Potiphar's wife. Who will Potiphar believe?

When have we found ourselves facing Potiphar's dilemma? Perhaps two children tell us opposing versions of who started an argument. Or two friends who are divorcing give their own version of whose behavior destroyed the marriage. How did we move forward in such situations?

Apparently, Potiphar is of two minds when deciding who is telling him the more accurate version of what happened while he was away. After all, he has the power to have Joseph killed if he wants to do so. Instead, Potiphar imprisons Joseph, but he is not sent to a maximum-security facility for hardened criminals. No, he is sent to a minimum-security prison where Pharaoh's men go when they are convicted of a crime. How do we know that? When Joseph arrives, the Pharaoh's baker and butler are already there.

When we experience a story from the perspective of each character, our perception of the story changes. We find ourselves asking different questions and putting ourselves in the shoes of unlikely characters—in this instance, Potiphar's wife. When we walk through the world of a story, looking over the shoulder or through the eyes of a character with whom we identify, we recognize the traits we have in common and the traits we would like to emulate. When we instead put ourselves in the shoes of a character with whom we would not immediately identify, we are confronted by the parts of ourselves that we would rather ignore or perhaps even reject. We learn about ourselves and about our world by journeying through the story in both ways, but we may learn more by exploring the character who exhibits traits we don't want to acknowledge in ourselves.

What Makes a Character a Sacred Presence?

A sacred character becomes a window into God and shows us what God is doing in the world. Throughout history, the church has chosen to name certain persons saints, but any person in our lives or any character in the stories we hear, read, or watch holds the potential of becoming a window into God for us. In the biblical narrative of Joseph, we are reminded again and again that Joseph makes his way in the world because "The LORD was with [him]" (Gen. 39:2).

Joseph is spoiled rotten as a child because he is the firstborn of his father Jacob's beloved wife Rachel. His father gives him a robe with long sleeves, meaning that Joseph doesn't have to take part in the hard work of his brothers, born to Jacob's other wife, Leah. This gives him a sense of entitlement that rubs his brothers the wrong way. To make matters worse, Joseph begins having dreams in which he is the most important figure and his brothers all serve (and even worship) him. He lords his life of privilege over his brothers, and, honestly, I would want to throw him in a hole or sell him to some passing tribe if he had been my brother. The young Joseph is an unlikely character to become a window into God. Perhaps that is why the storyteller continues reminding us that God's presence—not Joseph's charm—allows him to survive and even flourish in terrible circumstances.

Objects

Sometimes we don't pay them much attention, but the objects that appear in stories can hold great importance. They give a palpability or touchability to the world that the story is attempting to create. Some objects are absolutely necessary to the story, while others give our imagination additional information to consider. The cross in the Passion narratives of all four Gospels exemplifies a necessary object. Without the cross, we don't have a story! The spikes driven through Jesus' wrists and feet are necessary to the story as well. In contrast, the clothing that Simon of Cyrene wears or the objects that the women may have been holding as they watch and wait at the cross may not be necessary details, but they still add texture to the narrative of Jesus' crucifixion. We've probably all heard stories that were so heavy with detail that we became confused or overwhelmed and ceased to pay attention. Or stories that contained so few details that we had a difficult time entering the world of the story. An artful storyteller knows the importance of balancing necessary details with superfluous ones, making the experience real and rich for the listener or reader.

What Makes an Object Sacred?

We live our lives surrounded by objects—clothing, food, furniture, books, cars, and so on. Many of the items that surround us daily are disposable. They are intended for onetime use. So we use them and then recycle them or throw them away. Paper cups and plates are examples of onetime-use objects. Others are designed with "planned obsolescence" in mind. These objects will last for a limited amount of time, only to be thrown away and replaced later. Many household appliances fall into this category.

Some objects remain in our possession even after they have outlasted their usefulness, and we hold onto them for sentimental, emotional, or nostalgic reasons. We may not even know why we are keeping them or why they have created such a strong and lasting attachment. Many of these objects have stories connected to them. Perhaps we inherited them from a relative or they were given to us as a gift or we were in a certain location or with a special person when we purchased them. Whatever our reasons, we hang onto them. They have taken on a sacred value for us, even though we may not think of them in overtly religious terms. They become gifts of grace, and we see them as more than the ordinary, everyday objects that they appear to be to others. Perhaps they remind us of abiding love or hope—or even of the presence of God. But their stories alone do not make them sacred; instead, the stories open our awareness to the sacred gift of grace that is offered to us all. If we share the stories of these objects and how they became gifts of grace for us, those who hear the stories may recognize the presence of God.

Storytelling Prompts

1. With what biblical character do you identify? What about that character attracts you? How has identifying with that character formed your life and faith? Tell that character's story in first person—that is, as if you were him or her.

2. With whom can you share your personal stories? What about that person allows you to trust him or her? Which people in your life share their stories with you? What makes those relationships significant?

3. When has the mystery of life—the numinous—become clearly present for you, like it is for the narrator in

Robert Penn Warren's poem? The narrator points to the Divine by describing the sound of geese flying north. How would you describe your experience of the Divine?

CHAPTER 2

Finding the Sacred
in Your Story

The Cherry family home stood on a hill above Crockett's Creek about three miles from the town of Model in Stewart County, Tennessee. At the bottom of the hill and across the road was a pasture beside which Crockett's Creek ran, which, according to legend, had been named for the family of Davy Crockett. Across the creek stood the white-frame building that housed Crockett's Creek Baptist Church (founded in 1804, according to the sign nailed above the entrance). Down the opposite side of the hill was the Cherry family cemetery where at least four generations of that family had been laid to rest. My mother was born in this house, and my parents were living there at the time of my birth. I would have been born in the house had my mother not experienced life-threatening difficulties with her pregnancy. Instead, I was born at the hospital in Murray, Kentucky.

A porch on the front of the house looked down the long hill toward Crockett's Creek and the church, while another porch could be found at the back. The front door opened into a living room and beyond that a kitchen. In the living room, a naked light bulb swung loosely from the middle of the living room ceiling by a single black wire. The kitchen contained a large, crudely fashioned table surrounded by chairs, a refrigerator, and an electric range. In the 1950s, a bathroom was built on the back porch. It featured a footed tub, a sink, and a commode. This was the so-called "modern" side of the house.

My mother's family home was built on a floor plan common in the southeastern United States. A hall ran the length of the building, front to back, with rooms branching off each side. Off either side of the central hall were rooms defined either by their purpose or by the family member who slept there. The first room on the right was Dora's room. Dora was a first cousin to my mother, and we all called her Dori. Dori's immediate family had left the area around 1910 to claim land in the "Indian Territory" in what is now the state of Oklahoma. While her parents and all her siblings started a new life in the West, Dori elected to remain with her aunt—my grandmother. She never married and remained with our family until the day she died. By the time of Dori's death, my family had moved to Montgomery County, Tennessee, and the land on which my mother's home place stood had been taken by the Tennessee Valley Authority to create the Land Between the Lakes Recreation Area.

After my parents and I moved away from Crockett's Creek, we still visited the Cherry family home each Christmas. The Christmas tree stood in the living room. Fat red, blue, green, and yellow Christmas bulbs spiraled up the tree and gave the room its only truly festive décor. This was where we gathered in the evening before we were parceled off to different rooms at bedtime. I was sent to sleep with Dori in her room. What I remember most vividly about Dori's room was that it did not contain a stove. When I slept, I had so many quilts stacked on top of me that I felt in danger of being smothered to death from the weight. Even so, when I slipped beneath the sheet that lay atop the feather ticking mattress, it was so cold that I felt as though I were sliding under a sheet of ice. After what seemed like hours, my skinny torso began to generate a slight amount of heat. Once this precious warmth was created, my goal was to stay within the parameters of its cocoon. On Christmas Eve, Dori and I would stay up until the early hours of the morning in excited conversation about the presents we expected Santa to bring us. Sometimes other members of the household would open the door of Dori's room to tell us to keep our voices down, that other people were trying to sleep. That anyone could sleep while faced with the prospect of Santa's imminent arrival stretched our imaginations beyond their breaking point. Finally, sleep overtook us, and we entered the restless slumber of the expectant.

Dori and I woke before the sun rose, though she always seemed to awaken before me. At the time, I attributed her early-bird tendencies to her excitement about seeing what Santa had brought her. Now I realize that my Christmas joy caused me to be a restless sleeper, making me a less than ideal bedmate. We talked in whispers about how long we would allow the rest of the household to keep us from our presents. In truth, it wasn't long before we had awakened all our relations, most of whom were not as thrilled at the prospect of rising early as we were. Dori's room contained my memories of someone who not only allowed my childhood enthusiasm but also actively encouraged and took part in it.

The next room along that hallway belonged to the matriarch of the family, Minerva Chambers (formerly Minerva Cherry), my grandfather's sister. No one in the household called her by her given name. We simply referred to her as Aintie. She had been married for a brief time as a young woman, but whatever happened to Mr. Chambers was lost somewhere in that unnamed and unreachable cabinet where family members put topics they didn't want to discuss.

Aintie's room was a place of sanctuary for me from the large and powerful people who dominated the remaining rooms of the house. While the rest of the family members did what they thought was important—the farming and cooking and cleaning—Aintie and I sat on the front porch, looking down the hill toward Crockett's Creek. She told stories and sang ballads to me. Some of the stories were set in the early 1840s, during the time of my great-grandfather's boyhood, and others came from a time even earlier, during the initial settlement of that portion of land between the Cumberland and Tennessee Rivers. The ballads were those that the four Cherry brothers brought with them from the British Isles when they immigrated to North Carolina and later Tennessee. This spoken anthology of family history created an indelible bond between us.

I was "Aintie's boy," and I pretty much had the run of her room. Aintie's room contained a wood stove for heating, and next to that stove hung a charcoal portrait of the most beautiful woman I had ever seen: Minerva Cherry at sixteen. (Coincidentally, that was the age when she began to dip snuff.) Aintie's rocking chair stood nearby. She kept two pillows in her chair, one to sit on and one to support her back. I was so small at the time that I had to pull the pillows out of Aintie's chair into the floor in order to climb onto its seat. If someone caught and corrected me, I would simply tell them that it was Aintie's chair and I was Aintie's boy. I could do whatever I wanted with Aintie's pillows. I'm sure that attitude endeared me to the rest of the household. Aintie's bed stood against the wall opposite the stove, and when I had the rare privilege of sleeping in Aintie's room, we would stay up as late as we wanted and talk as loudly as we pleased. No one in that entire house was going to tell Aintie to be quiet. Aintie's room was as close to paradise as a small boy could ever hope for—at least it was for me.

Aintie's kitchen stood on the opposite side of the house from the modern kitchen, both rooms opening to the back porch. In the middle of Aintie's kitchen stood a rough wooden table with four straight-backed chairs. A dry sink sat against one wall and a wood cook stove sat against the other. In Aintie's kitchen, I learned to appreciate corn bread crumbled into a glass of buttermilk, a delicacy eaten directly from the glass with a spoon.

When fried chicken was on the menu, Aintie did not make a trip to the grocery store to find the fowl plucked, drawn, and quartered, resting in a Styrofoam coffin and wrapped in plastic for viewing. No, Aintie walked into the yard, taking her hatchet with her. When it came to killing chickens, Aintie was a chopper. As Aintie's helper, I served as part of the chopping crew, guided by the experienced hand of a woman who chopped wood for her stove into her eighties. First, she smoothed the feathers along the hen's neck. Then, with a swift, one-handed motion, she accomplished her purpose with deft accuracy. Often, in its headless rush toward death, the hen ran through the grass and wound up under the back porch, which was the shadowy home to all sorts of creeping, crawling life-forms. If that happened, I would have to crawl through the weeds and under the porch to retrieve our dinner. I was careful to see that this didn't happen. I had seen the creatures that lived under the porch and had no desire to meet them up close.

Aintie scalded and plucked the feathers from the unfortunate bird. She cut through the pale, prickled skin and yellow fat of the hen until she located the liver and gizzard. These would be fried and eaten, while the rest of the entrails would be thrown into the backyard for the dogs to enjoy. Once, I noticed a grayish-yellow, spongy-looking, oblong object inside the chicken. I asked Aintie what it was, and she replied that it was an egg. I knew what eggs looked like because I helped gather them from the henhouse. I had been taught to gently place them in a basket because they would break if they struck a hard surface—or sometimes even another egg. But this object, about the size and shape of an egg, looked as if it would bounce like a rubber ball rather than break. This was the egg before the hen laid it, the egg that had formed inside the hen. For the first time, there in Aintie's kitchen, I sensed that a hidden and protected region resided inside each living being—the place where the egg formed inside the hen or the place where secrets took residence in the human heart. Mystery lives at the center of each created being, and my encounter with that egg in Aintie's kitchen was the first time I recall being in the presence of that mystery.

Storytelling Prompts

1. Think of a place that is sacred to you. Is it a house, an apartment, or simply a room? Perhaps it is in the

woods, along a creek, or at the beach. Describe the place, giving as much detail as you can.

2. Who are the people that populate your sacred place? Describe their facial features, the clothes they wear, and anything else that distinguishes them. What did you learn from each person? How have your learnings been useful to you?

3. Describe your feelings associated with your sacred place and the people in it. How does your sacred place give you a sense of safety? What meaning do you find when you to return to your sacred place, either in person or in memory? Does your sacred place elicit a single feeling, or do you find yourself with mixed emotions?

Finding Your Windows into God

Since stories collect in places like houses or rooms or summer camps, they inevitably become attached to the people who inhabit those spaces. Those people with whom our most significant stories are associated become guiding lights for us. Certain people in our lives even become windows into God for us. Their stories open a divine encounter with the presence of God of which we may never catch a glimpse otherwise. That is why we call these people our *saints*.

In the Catholic tradition, the church defines who is considered a saint and who is not. Saint Paul calls any follower of Jesus a saint. Protestants, following Saint Paul's lead, think of every believer as one of the saints. For those of us who tell and hear stories, any person who gives us a glimpse of the Divine through his or her life becomes a saint for us. Here is the story of one of my saints.

When I was about three years old, my family moved from my mother's country home in Stewart County into the city of Clarksville, Tennessee, in neighboring Montgomery County. Both my parents had grown up in rural areas, so living in town was new for them. On Sunday afternoons, we would drive into the country, hoping to find a place outside of town where we could live. My dad would start up the 1946 Hudson, a car that looked as big as a house to my three-year-old self, and we would be on our way. My mother and father sat in the front seat while I sat in the back. Child restraints did not exist in those days—not even seat belts—so I often stood and leaned against the car window or the front seat and put my face between my father and mother.

As soon as my parents and I were far enough from home that my father would have been reluctant to turn around and go back, I got thirsty. I would complain to my father, "Daddy, I'm thirsty."

"You should have thought about that before you left home," he would answer.

"But I wasn't thirsty before I left home." A few moments later, I would continue. "Mama, I'm thirsty,"

"Listen to your father," she would reply.

This became our regular litany every time my parents and I went for a drive. Occasionally, my father would stop, and we would get a drink of water. On rare occasions, he would stop at a small cinder-block shop that sold soft-serve ice cream, and we would get more than a drink of water. I'm not sure he realized that those stops for ice cream only increased the likelihood of my getting thirsty the next time we went driving.

One Sunday afternoon, my parents and I piled into the Hudson and headed out of town. We crossed the Red River into a community called New Providence and turned onto a gravel road named Peacher's Mill Road. Perhaps because of the dust that the tires kicked up on the gravel road, I got thirsty. Thus began our litany.

"I'm thirsty."

"You should have thought about that before you left home."

"I wasn't thirsty before I left home. Mama, I'm thirsty."

"Listen to your father."

And on it went.

That particular Sunday, I pestered my father until he turned his eyes away from the road, looked directly at me in the back seat, and said, "Okay, the next house we come to, I'm going to stop and get you a drink of water. Are you satisfied?" Well, of course I was satisfied! I was getting what I wanted.

My father drove across an old, rickety bridge that passed over a railroad track, and we saw a house that was covered with asphalt shingles that were supposed to look like brick. In front of the house stood two large walnut trees. My father pulled the Hudson into the yard just beyond the second walnut tree, and my mother got out of the car and walked to the front door of the house to ask if her child could have a drink of water.

The woman who answered the door and spoke with my mother was somewhat ageless in my three-year-old eyes. She had hair that was the color of steel, tending toward silver rather than white. She wore a long cotton dress with a full apron covering the front. On her face were eyeglasses that had no rims, just gold earpieces and a gold nosepiece. She wore thick hose that I remember many other older women wearing during the early 1950s, and on her feet were a pair of heavy black shoes. After speaking with the woman for a brief time, my mother motioned for my father and me to come into the house. My father and I exited the car and met the owner, a woman named Kizie Butler.

Mrs. Butler showed us into her room, which contained a bed covered with a white chenille bedspread, a rocking chair with pillows on it that was clearly Mrs. Butler's chair, and several straight-backed chairs. Her chair reminded me of my Aintie's rocking chair, but this was not Aintie's room, so I made no move to sit in it. My parents and I sat in the straight-backed chairs. From where we were sitting, we could see what Mrs. Butler was doing in the kitchen—getting water from a bucket with a dipper. She did not have running water in the house. Instead, her water came from a pump above a cistern in the yard behind the house.

When I was growing up, people practiced an etiquette around buckets of water and dippers. With family members, everyone just drank after one another from the bowl of the dipper. When company came, however, glasses would be retrieved, and the water would be poured from the bowl of the dipper (from which the whole family drank) into the glasses. This practice was considered more sanitary. So Mrs. Butler retrieved three jelly glasses from the kitchen cupboard, and she filled two of the glasses almost full and the third about two-thirds full, all using the bowl of the dipper. She gave my parents the full glasses and me the partially full glass. Even then I considered this distribution of water to be unjust. After all, I was the one who was thirsty in the first place, and I had less water in my glass than the two adults had in theirs.

As I drank my water, Mrs. Butler talked to my parents, and we discovered during that conversation that Mrs. Butler only lived in half of her house. We didn't know that word *duplex* back then, but Mrs. Butler's house was built in a style similar to my mother's home place. Next to the room where we sat was a linoleum-covered hallway that ran the length of the house. Across that hallway was another half of the house, which was empty and available for rent. And thus, in a single afternoon, I got a drink of water, a new place to live, and a grandmother.

I had not known any of my grandparents since three had died before I was born, and my last grandmother, my mother's mother, died when I was nine months old. Mrs. Butler became my surrogate grandmother. She even encouraged me to call her Granny, though I didn't need any encouragement. She allowed me to stand on a small box in her kitchen and help her cook. I can only imagine how much help I really was.

When I got into trouble on my side of the house and received a whipping, all I had to do was make my way across the linoleum-covered hallway, and I was in safe territory. I would run into Granny's room crying, "Oh, Granny, wipe my tears, wipe my tears." She would stop whatever she was doing at the time, sit in her rocking chair, pick me up and put me on her lap, wipe my tears with her ever-present apron, and say, "What are they doing to my boy?" And I would tell her. I saw no reason to protect my parents. Her kindness gave Granny a special kind of authority in my three-year-old eyes. She was the person I sought out, for example, when my parents and I went to the store, and I talked them into buying me a book (which I attempted every time we went to the store). I would take my book to Granny's room for her to read it to me since I was too young to read myself.

Granny didn't have much formal schooling, and her pronunciation of certain words would have been considered "country." When Granny said the word *covers*, she

pronounced it *kivers*. When she said the word *help*, it
sounded like *hope*. But once I heard her read a book for
the first time, her original rendition of the story became
my holy writ. Anyone who read that book had to say *kivers*
and *hope* just like Granny had. She would tell me, "Now
Granny hasn't been to school very long. She doesn't always
know how to say the words right." But that didn't matter
to me. I knew that real authority did not come from giving
whippings; it came from wiping tears.

   This living arrangement went along as fine as fine could
be until one summer when Granny's biological grandchildren came to visit. Among them was a boy about my age
named Rusty. Rusty took it upon himself to set me straight.
He informed me that I was not Mrs. Butler's grandchild,
that I shouldn't call her Granny, and that I should stay on
my side of the house and stop bothering her so much. So I
did. I remained on my side of that linoleum-covered hallway, sitting in my little red rocking chair, and when I cried,
I did not have a soul to wipe my tears. Finally, though, the
car that had brought Rusty to the duplex took him away
again. Still, I wasn't sure whether to go back across the
hallway to visit Granny. After all, I knew I wasn't really
her grandchild. Perhaps I shouldn't be calling her Granny.
Perhaps I was bothering her too much.

   Not long after Rusty left, I heard heavy black shoes on
the linoleum in the hallway. The door on my side of the
house opened, and in came Mrs. Butler. I burst into tears
as soon as I saw her. (I should note that I had a relatively
happy childhood. I just cry a lot in this story.) She sat down,
held me in her lap, wiped my tears, and said, "What are
they doing to my boy?" I told her what Rusty had said—
that I wasn't her grandchild and shouldn't be calling her
Granny, that I should stay on my side of the house and stop

bothering her. She was quiet for a moment. Then, using both hands, she turned my face to look directly into hers and said, "Mike, I'm going to tell you something, and I don't want you ever to forget it. You are just as much my grandbaby as Rusty is, and don't you let anybody tell you any different."

A couple of years after Rusty's visit, my parents and I moved to Arizona, and following a three-year sojourn in the West, we moved back to Tennessee. When we first returned, we parked our trailer in a field across the road from Granny's house. A short time later, my father bought a half-acre of land across the river and moved our trailer there. We visited Granny occasionally, usually on a Sunday afternoon drive. Then, when I was sixteen years old, Granny died. I found myself in the funeral home, wearing the only suit I owned and surrounded by people I did not know. Some of her relatives were there, like her son, Kinslo. When I am feeling especially lacking in charity, I mention that Rusty was not in attendance. Actually, I mention that every time I tell this story. As I listened to people talk about Mrs. Butler, I noticed something. Even those who were not her blood relations were calling her Granny. At that moment, I realized that what she had been for me, she had been for a number of other people as well, and it was time for me to share.

Years later, as I was reading Revelation 21, the story of Granny came to mind. That chapter describes a God who wipes away all tears. When I read that passage, I saw Kizie Butler's hands. And it was Kizie Butler's face I saw, saying, "Yes, you are my very own grandbaby just like all the rest of these. Don't you let anybody tell you any different."

When I imagine that great banquet at the end of time—which I have always assumed would be a fish fry—I look with anticipation down the table to see the faces of those whom I loved and who loved me: my mother and father, my teachers and pastors, and Granny. But as I look down the table a little farther, whose face do I see? I see Rusty's face because my Granny was his Granny, she loved him too, and the table would not be complete for her without him there.

Storytelling Prompts

1. Think of someone who has been a window into God for you. Where did you first meet him or her? What did he or she look like? How did he or she sound? Describe him or her with as much detail as you can.
2. What were the surroundings in which you met this person—your home, his or her home, a school, a church, another setting? Describe the place with as much detail as you can.
3. What aspect of God did you come to see in this person's life? How do you feel when you remember this person? How has knowing him or her shaped your life and faith?

Finding Your Holy Relics

The summer after I turned eleven, my father decided to build a house out of cinder blocks behind my family's trailer. This little block house was twenty feet by twenty feet and was intended for my mother's washing machine, although she still chose to dry clothes on a clothesline. She claimed they smelled better that way. The little house would also come to serve as the storage place for the canned fruits and vegetables that my mother put up every summer in Ball-Mason jars. As the years passed, it also became a workshop for my dad, who was born with a native ability to repair nearly anything. He had been a mechanic for many years before he decided to take a correspondence course to study TV and radio repair. "The little house," as we came to call it, became a place to store any items we had no room for in the trailer.

Unfortunately, my father chose to begin this construction project about the time that I was beginning to realize that I knew everything and that he knew absolutely nothing. Perhaps many teens and preteens experience a similar moment of recognition with one or both of their parents. It was a difficult summer, given how hard it can be for someone who knows absolutely everything to work with someone who knows absolutely nothing, especially when the one who knows absolutely nothing thinks he's in charge. Every time I readied the cement mixture, which we called "mud," that went between the blocks, my father would come and add a little more water to it as if I had not done it correctly in the first place. Whenever I laid a row of blocks, my father would come and tap on the tops of one or two with the handle of the trowel as if I hadn't gotten them level. After I had run my finger between each row of blocks to make the indention that ran both vertically and horizontally, my father would come along and run his finger in those same grooves, as if my work was just not good enough. Did I mention that it was a difficult summer?

By the fall of that year, my father and I had put the roof on the cinder-block house and enclosed it so my mother could wash clothes there. Later that year, my dad experienced what in those days was politely called a "nervous breakdown." After fighting to get his so-called disability declared "service-related," he spent months in a veterans' hospital, and I knew in my heart that I had caused him to be there. Without anyone telling me so, I decided that my attitude and the arguments my father and I had that summer pushed him over the edge.

The hospital was in Murfreesboro, Tennessee, which was some distance from my home. My mother and I were only able to make a few trips there. During the months my father spent at the hospital, my mother and I faced several obstacles that kept us from visiting him on a regular basis. First, my mother did not drive an automobile, and I was not old enough to drive. Second, we did not have a telephone in our trailer. I had to walk across the road to a neighbor's house to borrow a phone to call my Aunt Sarah, my father's sister, to ask if she would take my mother and me to see him. These experiences may be why I have a difficult time asking people for help to this day. For someone who thought he knew everything, this experience taught me how little I really did know.

Finally, after many months, my father returned home. As he unpacked his suitcase, he pulled out a small, almost-square, brown object, turned to me, and said, "This is for you. I made it for you." I don't recall that my father had ever made anything for me before, but part of his treatment involved crafting objects out of leather. The brown leather object I held in my hand was a billfold, bound together with leather laces. On one side of the billfold, my father had tooled into the leather what appeared to be poinsettia leaves. The leaves were smooth against the textured leather, with berries in the middle. I turned over the billfold and saw that the other side had a laurel wreath tooled into the leather, and inside that wreath were my initials: MEW for

Michael Edward Williams. My father hadn't just made the billfold for me; he had personalized it.

Though I wouldn't have been able to articulate my feelings in these words at that age, I knew somewhere deep inside my soul that the billfold was a gift of grace. Someone who spent the time and effort to make something just for me—something with my initials tooled into it—even when I believed I was the person who sent him to the hospital in the first place, had offered a gift of grace.

I put the billfold in my pocket that very day. I didn't have anything to put in it other than a few school photos of my friends—mostly boys. Then after a few years, I added photos of girls and a few dollars and a driver's license. Then, in college, I added my university ID, more photos of young women, and even fewer dollars. Following that, I added graduate school IDs, a photo of one woman, business cards, credit cards, and just plain stuff. Over time, the poinsettia leaves, which always faced toward the outside of my pocket, were burnished to a high sheen. The laurel wreath and my initials, which faced the inside of my pocket, became dull and rough from the sweat that passed through the thin fabric of the pocket. After a while, the lacing that held the billfold together began to break, and the billfold could not stay in one piece. I was faced with a dilemma. I knew that my father would not replace the lacing in the billfold, and since this was the only project he ever made from leather, I felt that the process likely would serve only to unearth sad memories of his struggle with depression. I also knew the billfold wouldn't be the same if someone else fixed it, even me. So I took the gift of grace out of my pocket and placed it in a small wooden box for safekeeping.

Protestants don't usually talk much about relics, but we all have them. After my death, as my family goes through my personal effects, my daughters will find this worn and ragged billfold. Perhaps they will ask, "Why did Dad keep this old thing?" or "Why didn't he throw away this piece of junk?" Will they recognize that the billfold is a holy relic for me, a gift of grace? They certainly won't if they don't know the story behind it, which is why they have heard me tell it more times than they ever wanted.

Storytelling Prompts

1. What possession have you kept even after it outlived its use or purpose? Who gave it to you? What was the occasion or the circumstance of the gift?

2. When did you recognize this object as a gift of grace? What do you want others to know about the gift and its importance?

3. With whom do you need to share the stories that surround the holy relics in your life? Prepare your stories for each object, and set a time and place to tell them.

INTERLUDE: THE SECOND CREATION STORY

As someone finished telling the story of Creation where God declares that everything is good, a hand went up in the back of the room. One of the youngsters who had been listening to the story had a question.

"If everything's so good, how come there's homework?" It was the question of evil. It always arises.

Another hand shot up. "And Brussels sprouts?"

Then another. "And broccoli?"

Finally, a quiet, studious-looking young person raised a hand. "If everything is so good, how come people have to die?"

Well that's another story. When God is creating all that is, God takes some dirt. . . .

"I thought you said that God spoke everything into being!"

That was the first story, and this is the second. Pay attention.

"So where did God get the dirt?"

The Bible doesn't say, but some of the rabbis from ancient times believed that God asks angels to bring the dirt from the four corners of the world—some the color of rich black loam, some the color of coffee with cream, some the color of hot cocoa, and some the color of tea. Some is even white, chalky earth and some deep reddish clay. They say that God uses all the various colors of earth so no one can say, "My color of earth is holy, and yours is not." God gathers dirt from so many different places so that wherever people die—no matter how far away they are from where they were born—the earth will still receive them.

Anyway, God takes the dirt and makes a creature and names that creature *Adam*, which means "earthling" or maybe "dirt ball." We've all known a few dirt balls, haven't we? Let's give Adam the benefit of the doubt and say *earthling*. God places the earthling in a beautiful garden and tells Adam that any of the fruit from the trees in the garden is available for food—except for one. God forbids Adam from eating the fruit of the tree in the middle of the garden—the tree of the knowledge of good and evil. If Adam eats from that tree, death will be the result.

God enlists Adam in the work of naming the animals. We aren't sure how many names suggested by the earthling are actually approved by God, but at the end of the process, God says to Adam, "You know, it's not good for you to be alone. You can choose from any of the animals we just named to be your lifelong companion."

The choice is a difficult one. The elephant is so large and the tiger so fierce. Perhaps the duck? But no. Adam says to God, "I want someone just like me, only a little different. Just different enough to be interesting."

God says, "I know how you feel. I chose to make you, didn't I?

So God causes a deep sleep to fall upon Adam and takes some dirt from Adam's side. (The Hebrew word actually means "side," not necessarily "rib.") After all, what is Adam made from? Earth. God makes another creature exactly like the first, except a little different, just different enough to be interesting. For God, just as with any artist, no two pieces of art turn out exactly alike.

As soon as Adam spies the new creature, he—he is a he now—breaks into song. We don't know the tune, but we do have the words. He sings, "Bone of my bones and flesh of my flesh. You shall be called *ishah* ('woman') for I am called *ish* ('man')."

The two live together as companions, and they eat from every tree except the one in the middle of the garden—the tree of the knowledge of good and evil. They don't have to worry about what they are wearing because they wear no clothes and neither notices their own nakedness or the nakedness of their companion. Until one day, the new creature, who is called *Eve*, which means "The Mother of All That Lives," is walking through the garden and happens upon the serpent. Now, the serpent gets a bad reputation in later legend, but the Bible simply states that the serpent is the smartest creature in the garden. As Eve approaches the serpent, he asks her a question: "Why did God tell you not to eat from any of the trees in the garden?"

That is not what God said, so the woman corrects the serpent. "God said that we could eat from any of the trees of the garden, except for one. We cannot eat from the tree that stands in the middle of the garden. If we eat from it— even if we touch it—we will die."

Well, God hadn't said anything about not touching the tree. Perhaps the woman is just adding a layer of protection in following God's warning. After all, she can't eat what she doesn't touch.

"You won't die," the serpent tells her. "You will become like God."

Forgetting for a moment that she is already like God, the woman takes a bite of the fruit. It tastes good. She hands the fruit to Adam, and he takes a bite. Apparently he has been standing there all along without the wherewithal to enter the conversation. He thinks it tastes good as well. But something has changed for Eve and Adam. Something in the way Adam looks at Eve makes her decidedly uncomfortable. She covers her nakedness so he can't see it. Something about the way she looks at him makes him want to cover his nakedness as well. For the very first time, the two earthlings realize that they are naked, and they feel ashamed.

Adam and Eve attempt to make clothing but have no experience covering themselves. They choose the worst possible material: fig leaves. How uncomfortable was this clothing they made for themselves? Imagine choosing to make underwear from sandpaper and a skin irritant. So all Adam and Eve can do is scratch and hide from each other and from God.

Later that day, God walks though the garden in the cool of the evening, looking for someone with whom to share stories. God calls "Adam! Eve!" but no one answers. Finally, God locates the two earthlings by following the sound of scratching. They are hiding in the bushes. Adam emerges first. "Why didn't you tell us we were naked?" he asks. "You would think that would be an important thing to know."

At that moment, the universe falls silent. The only sound is the wrenching, grief-laden shattering of God's heart. "You did it, didn't you? You ate the fruit. Of all the trees in the garden, I only denied you one. You couldn't resist the fruit of that tree?"

"Well, the woman you gave me made me do it," says Adam, blaming Eve. God looks to Eve, and Eve tells God, "Well, the serpent tricked me." God looks to the serpent, but there is no one else to blame.

"You have no idea what you have done. As long as you were here with me, I could provide everything for you. But now you will have to leave the garden and provide for yourselves. You will have to work for what you have. You will have to set an alarm clock and get up early in the morning and work all day. When your work is done, you will not know whether you have accomplished anything. When you give birth to children, you will feel pain. And when they leave home, you will feel pain. And when they move back in with you . . . need I say more? Since you have made this decision on your own, you will have to make all your decisions from now on. I will be with you, but I will no longer make your choices for you. You have no idea what you've done."

So Adam and Eve prepare to leave the garden, packing their few itchy belongings. God, like a mother preparing her children for the first day of school, makes them clothes from the softest animal skins. Then, God watches as these two errant children leave the garden to make a life of their own, never to return.

That is why, my children, there is homework and broccoli and Brussels sprouts. And this is why each person who lives will taste death.

CHAPTER 3

The Paradox and the Journey

Though perhaps difficult to see at first glance, the two Creation stories of Genesis do share similar themes. They both tell us that humans can experience the sacred in their encounters with nature and one another. They both explain that each of us is a unique work of art made by a master artist and that we bear the stamp of God's image. Still, they are wildly different stories. Each one emphasizes a particular understanding of who God is and the nature of the universe.

In the first Creation story, God, the storyteller, speaks the world into being. We witness God's playful enjoyment in seeing what will happen next and how each specific part of creation will look and sound. God watches each new part of the universe appear with divine surprise and delight. The deep delight that God takes in watching the story of Creation unfold is underscored every time God sees that the next line of the story is either good or very good. Toward the close of that first rendition of Creation, God speaks into being creatures who are like God—similar enough to continue telling the story of Creation and even be a part of its continuous becoming. Humans are enough like God to have a relationship with their Creator. At the end of the first story of Creation, we understand that everything in the universe is good because God created it and declared it so.

The second story of Creation is strikingly different. While God still performs the role of an artist in this narrative, God acts as a sculptor, making a human out of the earth that apparently has already been created. We pick up the story in the middle of the process of Creation, right at the point when humans appear. God uses dirt, the most ordinary substance in the world, and the earthling doesn't take on life until God breathes divine breath into it. In this second narrative, one earthling is created at a time, in contrast to the first story, in which male and female appear at the same time.

In the second telling of Creation, the single earthling, named *Adam* for the substance from which it was sculpted, is given a garden in which to live and every fruit from every tree in the garden (except one, of course) to eat. When God denies Adam the fruit of the one tree, we as human beings can almost predict what will happen. We always want the very thing denied us. If we are told that we can look in any room of a house but one, which room most draws our attention? This story represents a flawless portrayal of our shared human nature.

Adam takes part in naming the other creatures, and God sees that this creature of earth will not be fulfilled by divine company alone but will need another creature made of earth for companionship. Then God is described as a kind of surgeon-sculptor, causing a deep sleep to fall on

Adam. From the dirt of Adam's side, God makes a second creature. Each creation is different from the other—one of a kind. Some commentators suggest that the dirt to make Adam's companion was taken from his side rather than his head or feet so that one creature will not rule over the other but live as true companions, sharing a life together among the beauty and the fruits of the garden.

So far, though the details of the two Creation stories differ, the idea that everything is good drives both narratives. That essential goodness, however, is about to change. Enter the serpent. In later centuries, the serpent has come to be identified as Satan—a force for evil. As far as we can tell, however, the idea that a second force existed in the universe equal to or just a little less powerful than God was not present in Israel's thinking from the start but later imported from Persia. In this story, the serpent is described as smart or shrewd, a creature whose only influence lay in its power of persuasion and deception.

The serpent begins by suggesting that God has been miserly about the fruit in the garden by not allowing the earthlings to eat from any of the trees. Eve corrects that misconception—they can eat from any tree except for the tree of the knowledge of good and evil—but exaggerates, saying that she and Adam are forbidden to touch the tree as well. The serpent asserts that eating the one forbidden fruit will not lead to death but to a godlike status for the humans. Of course, both earthlings eat the fruit the serpent offers and, while its taste is sweet, it possesses what we would call side effects. Among the fruit's unforeseen consequences for the humans is the recognition of their nakedness and a sense of shame when they see each other unclothed. They hide from each other and from God.

Adam's and Eve's ineptness at making clothing for themselves is as laughable as it is predictable. After all, they have never had to cover themselves before. Where they had once seen in each other the same beauty as the grass and trees and other creatures with whom they share the garden, now they feel ashamed when they look at each other.

The earthlings fall into decision-making. After they decide to eat the forbidden fruit, they continue to make one decision after another. And with the freedom to make decisions comes the potential that the results of those decisions will be destructive as well as creative. Some say this story parallels the psychological development of the individual human being. Children grow to the point that they begin to make decisions for themselves, and with that stage of life comes the unforeseen consequences of each decision.

Adam and Eve don't fall down dead as soon as they eat the fruit, but now they will die—eventually. For human life to continue, they will have to reproduce. And other humans coming into the world create an even greater potential for both creative and destructive results. In fact, each decision we make as human beings holds the potential to produce not just creativity or destruction but both.

The editor who chose to put these very different stories of Creation side by side at the opening of Genesis knew that to tell the truth, the whole truth, and nothing but the truth, we must tell more than one story. This decision was an act of metaphoric imagination. Poets employ metaphors to compare something we know well to something we don't know. Jesus employs metaphors from everyday life to give readers a hint at the nature of God. When Jesus begins a story with, "The kingdom of God is like . . . ," he invites the listener to employ that same metaphorical imagination. The parables of Jesus are extended metaphors that startle us out of our expected reality and show us a new way to experience what God is doing in the world.

The Greek word *parabola*, from which we get the English word *parable*, literally means to throw one thing down next to another. When Jesus tells a story that places the reality of God's activity in the world next to the ordinary reality of his listeners' lives, he gives us a glimpse into how we might fit into God's kingdom. In doing so, he engages our parabolic imagination.

When the editor of Genesis places those two radically different stories of Creation side by side, we are invited into that same metaphoric or parabolic imagination that Jesus exercises. The first Creation story asserts that everything is good because God created it, which is true. The second Creation story asserts with equal force that everything is broken, and we humans are the ones who broke it, which is also true. When two equally accurate stories offering opposite assessments of a situation are juxtaposed, we move beyond a simple metaphor or parable. We have moved into the realm of *paradox*. Creation is both good and broken at the same time. Paradox creates a tension that emerges at the heart of divine encounter and spiritual exploration. We see this paradox in the stories of Abraham, Sarah, Moses, and Miriam, who find themselves separated from their homeland. Some are called to leave, and others are taken away unwillingly from all they know. Later, their descendants are taken into captivity in Babylon, and their sole place of worship is destroyed. They are both chosen and exiled at the same time. This paradox produces prophets before, during, and after the exile, and their prophetic visions and utterances emerge from that tension. The early followers of Jesus also live with such a paradox when they not only believe the proclamation that Jesus is God's chosen one but also witness Jesus being tortured, humiliated, and executed as a criminal, all acts that seemingly disqualify him from being the Son of God. The tension of living between those two paradoxical stories produces the letters, Gospels, and visions that are collected in the New Testament.

At the core of the scriptures, we find the deep insight that truth is far more complex than any one perspective can contain or express. Scripture employs metaphor, parable, and paradox to add depth to our stories and to enlarge our view of who God is and what God is doing in the world. This is not complexity for complexity's sake; the reality of God is greater than what we as humans can understand. Metaphor, parable, and paradox acknowledge our human limitations while at the same time offering us a means of transcending them.

———

God's Grandeur

The world is charged with the grandeur of God.
It will flame out, like shining from shook foil;
It gathers to a greatness, like the ooze of oil
Crushed. Why do men then now not reck his rod?
Generations have trod, have trod, have trod;
And all is seared with trade; bleared, smeared
      with toil;
And wears man's smudge and shares man's
      smell: the soil
Is bare now, nor can foot feel, being shod.

And for all this, nature is never spent;
There lives the dearest freshness deep down
      things;

And though the last lights off the black West went
Oh, morning, at the brown brink eastward,
    springs—
Because the Holy Ghost over the bent
World broods with warm breast and with ah!
    bright wings.
                    —Gerard Manley Hopkins*

The year is 1877. A young man sits down to write a poem.
He had given up such endeavors for a number of years
because he thought it detracted from his journey of faith.
Now, however, he is convinced that he can express the
insights from his journey in no better way. He begins with
the following words: "The world is charged with the grandeur of God." These words define the very basis of his spiritual exploration. There is nowhere he can go where God is
not. All of creation reflects God's grandeur.

This poem was not the beginning of Gerard Manley
Hopkins's spiritual or artistic exploring. He had grown
up in an Anglican household, and his interest in poetry
began early. In fact, he had won the poetry prize at High-
gate School seventeen years earlier. His education continued at Balliol College, Oxford, where he graduated with
first-class honors. At Oxford, he came under the influence
of John Henry Newman, who had written about his own
journey from the Anglican Church to Roman Catholi-
cism in his book *Apologia Pro Vita Sua*. Hopkins read this
book and, influenced by Newman's thought, converted to
the Roman Catholic Church in 1866. This choice cut him
off from many of his family and friends. The next year, he

*Gerard Manley Hopkins, "God's Grandeur," *The Poems of Gerard
Manley Hopkins* (Oxford: Oxford UP, 1948), 70.

decided to enter the Society of Jesus, and that was when he
began abstaining from writing poetry unless his superiors
ordered him to do so. By the year of his ordination in 1877,
the same year he wrote "God's Grandeur," Hopkins had
started writing again.

Hopkins would continue his spiritual exploration
through a series of parishes in Oxford, Liverpool, Glasgow,
London, and other cities in England until 1884 when he
was named Professor of Classics at University College,
Dublin. In addition to teaching classes in Latin and Greek
at the university, he continued to struggle with his religious
and artistic callings until his death in 1889.

Hopkins lived in the tension between his divine
encounters with God's grandeur and his gift with words
and images. He vacillated between rejecting his calling as a
poet to fully embrace his religious commitments and using
his poetic gifts as a means of exploring and expressing his
religious journey. This tension meant that a volume of Hopkins's poems would not be published until 1918, when Robert Bridges, a friend from Oxford, shepherded a collection
of the late priest-poet's work into print.

Hopkins's last years were filled with a heavy load of
teaching and grading exams. He was prone to emotional
struggles and bouts of depression. Supposedly, he told
those with him how happy he was when he was dying. Of
course, we can speculate that his happiness came from the
prospect of being with the God he had served and to whose
constant presence he testified in his poetry. Perhaps death
simply confirmed his poetic intuition of divine encounter
as summed up at the end of his poem: "Because the Holy
Ghost over the bent / World broods with warm breast and
with ah! bright wings."

The Spiritual Journey

We are all on a spiritual journey. Yes, just as we are all storytellers, whether we know it or not, so we are all on a spiritual journey, though many of us are not aware of it. Everything that we experience in life forms us—both the things we do and the things that are done to us. For the most part, we are unaware of the many ways that our experiences form us in body, mind, and spirit.

The dynamic metaphor of the journey is one of the most ancient images for life. We are moved to tell each other stories in part because we have been apart from each other, one or the other or both on a journey. We share with others what happened (what events were forming us) from the simple need to be known and understood. Abraham and Sarah are sent by God on a journey to a place they have never heard of. There is no question that the experiences they have on their journey shape their lives and shared faith—along with the lives and faith of their descendants.

A journey is the primary feature of many ancient and modern stories. Gilgamesh travels to speak with Utnapishtim (the survivor of the great flood) in the epic that takes its name from its primary character. Odysseus travels home after fighting a war, and his adventures are recorded in a narrative named for him as well. The Gospels tell a variety of stories that center on the lives of a man named Jesus and his disciples as they journey between Galilee and Judea and then toward Jerusalem, where Jesus meets his arrest, trial, crucifixion, and resurrection.

The metaphor of journey holds significance because it concretely describes inner transformation through external movement. We might say, "I'm not in the same place that I was when I was a child or teenager or young adult," meaning that our thoughts and attitudes about life, love, what is important, or any number of other things have changed. If we are "not in the same place," then we have been on a journey.

All of life is an opportunity to travel through a world that is "charged with the glory of God." Because of God's omnipresence, each journey has the potential to be a spiritual journey. We can catch glimmers of God's presence "like shining from shook foil" in even the most ordinary settings—from people we meet every day and in objects that no one else would consider extraordinary. When we take the time to reflect on the journey of life, we can feel God's presence as it "gathers to a greatness" all around us, embracing us with divine love. We are free to explore the frontiers of our lives and the world because there is no place we can travel that is bereft of God. Our spiritual journey becomes a means of exploring our own lives as we tell the stories of those persons, places, and things that have shaped us as children of God. May we journey with faith and confidence in God's love and continuing presence with us.

Storytelling Prompts

1. Tell a story of a time when you experienced creation as good. Then, tell a story of a time when you experienced creation as broken. Finally, tell a story of a time when you experienced the goodness and brokenness of creation simultaneously.

2. When, if ever, have you felt the tension between your faith and your career as Hopkins did? Tell a story of a time when you had to choose between your life of

faith and the demands of your job. How could you have woven your faith and career together so that each one supported and enhanced the other?

3. When have you seen "God's grandeur" in your life or the life of someone else? Describe how you experienced God's presence in that moment.

CHAPTER 4

Stories of Fear, Fantasy, and Faith

We live between the stories of the Garden and the Exile. The tension between these stories sends us on our journey of spiritual exploration. If we refuse to break the tension and don't give ourselves over to either the fear of the prospect of death or the fantasy of the utopian dream of returning to the garden, then we are ready to begin our voyage of discovery. When we resist minimizing God's story to a story of fear or to a story of fantasy, we can embark on the surprising journey beyond fear and fantasy.

The story of fear asks, *What if something tragic happens? What if my dream life turns out all wrong, different from the way I imagined it? What if the very worst thing that could happen does happen?* Sometimes fear stops us in our tracks and makes us unable to address our current situation or stand up for ourselves and others. Nevertheless, fear can be a great motivator—oftentimes to negative effect. Fear is one of the most forceful tools used by political and religious figures to gain power over large groups of people. Make them afraid, tell them who they should fear, then provide the solution to their fear, and anyone can gain people's allegiance. Unfortunately, such "solutions" usually include some form of slavery, oppression, or genocide. Stories of fear can convince us that the world is a singularly dangerous place and that everyone different from us poses a threat.

This does not mean that there are not occasions in which fear is a reasonable response. Fear can assist us in avoiding dangerous situations and keep us from taking unnecessary risks. Stories of fear may keep us from driving too fast or eating or drinking some unidentified substance or approaching a bear in the wild. Stories of fear can function to keep us safe, but they can also keep us from attempting to become friends with someone because he or she looks different, speaks another language, or comes from another country. Reasonable fears protect us from harm, while unreasonable fears become unhealthy when they keep us from experiencing our lives in rich and exciting ways and lead us to harm others.

The story of fantasy, on the other hand, asks, *What if something wonderful happens to me? What if my life can be made perfect? What if I can return to the idyllic state that the two first humans knew in Eden?* This is the story that utopians tell and try to hold on to, wanting to replicate life in the Garden of Eden by creating a sort of heaven on earth. In most cases, these utopian experiments turn out to be dystopias—earthly heavens that quickly turn into hells. Or they simply fizzle out, losing the energy it takes to keep up the pretense that "Every day, in every way, [things are] getting better and better."

This is not to say that it is wrong to have dreams or to imagine a better future. It is next to impossible to work toward better life conditions unless we can imagine what they might look like. Both coaches and stage directors know the power of the athlete or performer invoking the power of imagination to prepare for a sporting event or a role in a play. Imagination can be a powerful means of preparing ourselves for an upcoming interview, a difficult conversation, a proposal of marriage, and any number of other significant life events. Stories of fantasy become a problem when they disconnect us from the reality of our lives, when they cease to prepare us for the future, when they become an alternate reality in which we live, and when they hinder our ability to act.

We learn early to tell ourselves stories of fear and fantasy in part because they create a certain energy in our bodies and psyches. Stories of fear tap into that ancient part of our brain that houses our fight-or-flight instincts. When in fight-or-flight mode, our respiration increases, and the muscles of our chest tighten. We may feel as though our hearts are in our throats. Fear energizes us to do something (run away or strike out verbally or physically), even if what we do promises to make the situation worse. Over and over, Jesus tells his disciples not to be afraid—not because scary people and frightening occasions don't exist but because Jesus understands the kind of people that fear turns us into. Fear can turn us into people who are either timid or cruel. Understandably, Jesus didn't want his disciples to be either.

Fantasy stories tend to engage our imaginations in speculation, often leading us to compare ourselves to others. We dream of having exorbitant amounts of money and living in a large and expensive house like the ones we see on television. Or we long for bodies like those we see gracing the covers of fashion magazines and clothes like those worn by models. We do this even after we have learned that those photos have been altered and do not represent the real person but an idealized, completely false, and unreachable image of the human form. Sometimes we yearn for all of the above—the money, the looks, and the lifestyle of celebrity performers, athletes, and even those who are famous for just being famous. The ancient word for the energy stimulated by fantasy stories is *covetousness.*

As we move along our spiritual journeys, we live in the tension between fear and fantasy. But I know of a third way to continue our spiritual journeys: We can choose to live a story of faith and trust in God and God's goodness. Making this choice does not mean that we will never feel fear or submit to fantasies about the future. Stories of faith do not resolve this tension; instead, they help us transcend fear and fantasy in surprising ways by pointing toward the divine presence in our lives.

The rest of this chapter will draw upon stories from my life as well as stories from the Joseph saga found in Genesis. These stories will offer examples of how living in the tension between stories of fear and fantasy can move us toward the trust that comes from encounters with the Divine and transform those stories of fear and fantasy into stories of faith.

My Spiritual Journey
Episode 1: Tornado

One afternoon in 1998, a tornado passed through Nashville. I was working in my office at church, oblivious to the threatening weather outside. Finally, my wife, Margaret, called me and asked if I expected her to pick up our older daughter, Sarah, from elementary school or if I was planning to do it.

"Why?" I asked.

"Have you looked outside?" she responded.

When I did, I saw a darkened and stormy sky and leaves and branches of trees being twisted and blown about by violent winds. "I'll be right home," I told her.

On my way home, the wind was blowing the street signs from side to side. As I turned to drive up the hill toward my street, a tree limb fell directly in front of my car, causing me to stop suddenly but not before I had driven on top of the limb. As I reversed the car off the limb and started back up the hill, I thought, *Here I am, three blocks from home, and I'm going to die!* When I arrived at my house, I discovered that a limb had fallen from one of the Bradford pear trees in the front yard and was blocking the driveway. I had barely enough room to get my car off the street. I ran inside and found Margaret and our younger daughter, Elizabeth, in the basement. I joined them there and could feel a pain in my head as the pressure changed inside our house because of the tornado passing over.

Finally, when I determined that it was safe to go outside, I walked to the school to pick up Sarah. The wind had knocked down large trees all over the neighborhood, and two of them were blocking each end of the street that offered access to the elementary school. The buses that normally lined up in front of the school each afternoon could not reach it. The electricity was out in the neighborhood and throughout most of the city as well. I walked into the darkened front hallway of the school where children were lined up along its length with their heads tucked toward the wall and their little backsides sticking up. I found Sarah's class, and she was released to me by her teacher. Many of her classmates did not arrive home until much later that night.

As I sat at my computer in my office that afternoon, oblivious to the storm outside, I was living out the fantasy that all was right in the world. As soon as I looked outside and saw the dangerous configuration of dark clouds, I felt only fear for myself and my family. That fear intensified as I traveled the three miles between the church and my house. *What if something has already happened to Margaret or Sarah or Elizabeth? What if I can't get to them? What if I can do nothing to help them?* These are the questions I asked myself. Though my fear was natural and understandable, none of my fears came to pass.

Don't get me wrong. This story could have turned out quite differently. Especially in times of natural or human-made disasters, people are sometimes harmed, even killed. My story of fear might have come true. Does that mean that I would have acted differently in the situation? Probably not. My trust is not in the outcome of the story but in the One who accompanies me through the story, no matter the outcome. Trusting in the divine presence is not an insurance policy against tragedy. It is, however, the assurance that we do not walk through tragedy alone but are accompanied by a God who knows loss and grief and knows us better than we know ourselves.

Storytelling Prompts

1. Think of a celebrity, sports figure, musician, or a person from history who you would like to be. How did you come to learn about this person? What makes you

admire him or her? What qualities or traits does he or she possess that you would like to emulate? Then think about yourself as someone other people look up to and aspire to be. Tell a story about why people might want to be you.

2. Recount a time when you or someone you love were in physical danger or a time when you thought you or someone you love were in physical danger. Use the skill you have learned to describe the world of your surroundings, the people who were with you, and the objects that were important to the story. How did this encounter affect and change you? If you find yourself struggling to think of a story, remember that you don't need an experience of a tornado passing through your neighborhood to feel fear.

My Spiritual Journey
Episode 2: Illness

I am an only child. My mother miscarried several times before I was born, and doctors warned her not to try to have another child. She ignored their advice and, though she carried me to term, had such a difficult pregnancy that she was forced to go to the hospital in Murray, Kentucky, to give birth. My father remained at the hospital with her, sleeping in the waiting room chairs in case I was born with issues that required a blood transfusion.

I was a sickly child from the start, causing constant work and worry for both my parents. They took me from doctor to doctor to discover the root of my almost constant ill health. This story of fear—that my parents' only child would die—drove my family's narrative. Finally, when I was five years old, my parents decided to move to a climate that would better suit my sickly constitution. Doctors had told them that the dry air of the desert often worked wonders for someone who suffered from symptoms like mine, even though these same doctors could not put a name to the malady from which I suffered.

At that time, my father was working as a mechanic at the motor pool at Fort Campbell, Kentucky. He arranged for a transfer to Fort Huachuca, Arizona, at the very southernmost part of the state in the desert near the town of Sierra Vista. My parents eagerly pursued the fantasy that the desert air would work a miracle and that my health would improve dramatically. When we arrived in Arizona, we lived in rented trailers until my dad could earn enough to buy a trailer of our own. My health did improve slightly, but it was not the dramatic improvement for which my parents had hoped. They moved from the fantasy of miraculous cure back into the fear of a premature death.

Once again, my parents took me to doctor after doctor in Arizona with the same results we had gotten in Tennessee. In desperation, they sought out a new pediatrician in town, Dr. Howard Robertson. Dr. Robertson had retired from teaching at Vanderbilt Medical School, an institution that was fewer than fifty miles from our previous home in Tennessee. We were told that he had come to Sierra Vista and set up a pediatric practice at the request of the commanding general at Fort Huachuca who had grandchildren living in the area at the time.

Almost immediately, my parents and I built trust with Dr. Robertson and his wife, who served as the nurse in the practice. He had a wonderful way with children. (That first day we met, he began to call me "Hoss" and "Professa" in his gracious Alabama accent and continued to address me in that manner as long as I was his patient.) Dr. Robertson concerned himself not only with my physical health but also with my psychological health. I had struggled with the transition from my school in Tennessee to the school in Arizona in the middle of my first-grade year. One of the first questions he asked my parents was, "Who is making this child so afraid?" In truth, the story of fear had so overtaken my psyche that pretty much everything made me anxious and afraid.

After Dr. Robertson had examined me several times and looked over my past medical records, he decided to send me to a large medical center in Tucson for tests. There were several possibilities for a diagnosis, some of them so dire as to be life-threatening. Dr. Robertson didn't tell my parents about the worst of these diagnoses until later, nor did he reveal that he would lie awake at night, wondering if he could keep me alive long enough to find out what was wrong with me. My most vivid memory from that time was that several of the tests required that I take large doses (at least they seemed outrageously large to me) of castor oil in preparation for them. I hated the taste, which reminded me of the smell of motor oil, and I gagged at the consistency, almost unable to drink it and keep it down.

Dr. Robertson received my test results from the hospital in Tucson, and he shared them with my parents and me, letting us know that his worst fears were not realized. I had been born with a blood deficiency that affected my immune system. This problem had only recently been discovered, so Dr. Robertson had consulted with his former colleague at Vanderbilt Medical School, Dr. Amos Christie. His association with Dr. Christie was the reason he thought to test for that particular deficiency. My deficiency could be treated by injections of gamma globulin—nine cc's every six weeks. Gamma globulin is very thick, meaning the injections were given slowly and were more painful than ordinary injections. Over time, though, and with continued treatment, I grew into an active and healthy young person for the first time in my life.

Storytelling Prompts

1. When have you feared for the health of a family member—a child, parent, or sibling—or even a close friend? How would you describe the way the fear manifested itself in your body? Did your throat get tight or your stomach hurt? Did you feel tension in your muscles? Did the fear move you to act or stop you from acting? What helped you cope with the fear?
2. Tell a story about a hope you have for the future of someone you love. Or think back to dreams you had for yourself when you were younger. Perhaps you dreamed of attending a certain college, attaining a dream job, or finding the ideal mate. Did you attend that college, get that job, or develop a relationship with that person? If not, describe the disappointment you felt when you learned that your fantasy was not going to be realized. Describe any good that resulted from your disappointment. Craft a story that explains how you didn't get what you wanted and made the best of it.
3. If you did get to attend that college, were hired for that dream job, or had a relationship with that ideal person, tell a story about a time when you got what you wanted and it didn't turn out the way your fantasy led you to believe it would.

Joseph's Spiritual Journey
Episode 1: Exclusion

Though we experience stories of fear and fantasy in our own lives, we also read them in the Bible. One such example can be found in the Joseph saga in Genesis 37–50. We have already considered the episode of Joseph's story that takes place in Potiphar's house as an example of the importance of character. Joseph's father, Jacob, grew up as the favored child of his mother, Rebekah. Jacob, in turn, favors Joseph, the child of his beloved wife, Rachel, for whose hand in marriage Jacob worked for fourteen years. The fact that Jacob's brother, Esau, was his father's favorite and Jacob was his mother's favorite led to such heartache and hatred between the brothers that Jacob had to leave home because of Esau's threats on his life. One would think Jacob had learned the damage that playing favorites among children could cause, yet he repeats the pattern of his parents with a similar result.

Jacob not only favors Joseph over Rachel's other child but also over the sons of his other wife, Leah, and over the sons of his wives' slaves. We see evidence of that favoritism in the coat that Jacob gives to Joseph—a coat with long sleeves. When I first heard this story, the coat was described as having many colors. No doubt it was a beautiful coat and fancier than anything owned by the other brothers, but the long sleeves indicate something even more telling. The coat with long sleeves prohibits Joseph from doing any of the shepherding work required of his brothers. In fact, his favored status only adds to his brothers' workload since he doesn't contribute his share. Perhaps Jacob's favoritism toward the son of his beloved wife betrays his fear that he will lose Joseph. After all, the work of keeping flocks could be dangerous to the shepherd as well as the sheep.

Joseph lives in a fantasy world of his own grandeur. He has a dream about gathering grain in a field with his brothers—an unlikely dream since Joseph seems allergic to that kind of hard work! In this dream, his brothers' sheaves of grain bow down to his. In another dream, the sun, moon, and stars bow down to the great and magnificent Joseph. Joseph not only lives in a fantasy world of great dreams but also exercises such poor judgment that he tells his brothers about his dreams of their subservience to him. They grow to hate him more and more with each new dream.

Finally, Joseph is sent to take food to his brothers while they are keeping their father's sheep. First, Joseph is portrayed as being so clueless that he has difficulty even finding his brothers. They see him coming, and they plot about what they might do to "this dreamer." Joseph's brothers throw him in a pit, and he is sold to (or discovered by, depending on the tradition) a caravan that then sells him as a slave to one of the officers of the King of Egypt, a man named Potiphar. The brothers then dip Joseph's long-sleeved coat into the blood of a goat and take it back to their father, telling him they found it and allowing him to believe his beloved son had been devoured by some wild animal. Jacob's story of fear has come to pass; Rachel's son is gone forever.

Storytelling Prompts

1. Tell a story about a time when you felt excluded from your family, a group of friends, or even a church group. How did the exclusion make you feel? Consider any

good that resulted from your experience of being left out. How were you aware of God's presence during this time "in the pit"?

2. Tell a story about a time when you were part of a group, family, club, or congregation that excluded others. Did you act as a leader or as a bystander? Did you speak up for or against the exclusion? How did you feel when you spoke one way or the other? While telling your story, put yourself in the shoes of the excluded people. How did they feel? How were you aware or unaware of God's presence during that time?

Joseph's Spiritual Journey
Episode 2: Accusation

Joseph's dreams of grandeur do not seem to be coming to pass. He is a slave in the household of a wealthy Egyptian. Despite all evidence to the contrary, the biblical storyteller informs us that God is with Joseph. Soon enough, Joseph rises to the level of chief steward in Potiphar's house, second in power only to his master. Because of Joseph's position, Potiphar's wife begins to take notice of the young Hebrew slave. Whenever her husband is away on business, she propositions Joseph, suggesting that the two of them become lovers. Aware of his status as a slave and the trust his master has placed in his integrity, Joseph refuses her advances. This angers Potiphar's wife, who is apparently not used to being refused anything that she wants, and she plots to destroy Joseph.

One day, when Joseph and Potiphar's wife are alone in the house, she again makes sexual advances toward the young slave, and he rebuffs them. As she insists that he do

with her what she desires, Joseph makes his escape by slipping out of his outer garment—his coat. In her intense anger
at being rejected repeatedly, Potiphar's wife announces to
everyone in the household that Joseph has tried to sexually
assault her and presents his coat as evidence. Coats always
seem to be getting Joseph into trouble. Upon his master's
return, Joseph is imprisoned.

As I mentioned in chapter 1, Joseph is not put to death,
although I am quite sure that Potiphar, one of Pharaoh's
high officials, could have ordered his execution. Instead,
he is imprisoned in what might be considered little more
than house arrest. Why such a light punishment for a seri-
ous charge? Perhaps Potiphar doubts his wife's accusa-
tion that Joseph assaulted her. After all, he has trusted the
young Hebrew slave with his entire household. Potiphar
must consider Joseph supremely trustworthy. Or perhaps,
as the biblical storyteller indicates, Joseph receives a lesser
punishment because God is with him even as he is falsely
accused, convicted, and imprisoned. This is certainly not
a fantasy story, having nothing to do with the grandiose
dreams of Joseph's childhood. Still, the storyteller refuses
to allow the story to become one of fear, asserting that God
accompanies Joseph through his hardships and still works
with him for good.

Storytelling Prompts

1. Tell a story of a time when you were accused of something you didn't do. Where did it take place, and who
   were the persons involved? How did it feel to be falsely
   accused? Did you defend yourself or remain silent? In

what ways were you aware or unaware of God's presence during this time?

2. Tell a story of a time when you falsely accused someone
   else—perhaps through sharing a piece of gossip before
   checking its authenticity. Even if you later found out
   that the information was incorrect and tried to change
   the story, you still hurt another person. How did it feel
   to hurt someone else, even if you never intended to
   do so? How could you have attempted to correct the
   information or make amends to the person who was
   hurt? How were you aware of God's presence during
   this time?

Joseph's Spiritual Journey
Episode 3: Forgetting and
Remembering

As he had in Potiphar's household, Joseph soon rises to
become the most trusted among all the prisoners. After a
time, Pharaoh's imprisoned servants begin to have dreams,
and Joseph offers to interpret them with God's help. Joseph
tells the servants that God is the true interpreter of dreams.
The cupbearer dreams of a vine with three branches, all
of which blossom and produce clusters of grapes. In the
dream, he takes the grapes, presses them into Pharaoh's
cup, and then hands the cup to the king. Joseph tells the
cupbearer that his dream means that he will be restored to
Pharaoh's service in three days. Joseph also asks that he not
forget him once he is back in Pharaoh's favor.

The baker, who has also been having dreams, is excited
to hear the positive interpretation of the cupbearer's dream

so he is eager to tell Joseph about his own. He dreams that he has three baskets on his head and that the top basket contains different kinds of baked goods. To the baker's dismay, birds begin eating the baked goods. Joseph tells the baker that in three days, Pharaoh will lift the baker's head from his body and that birds will pick the flesh from his severed head. Not the interpretation the baker is hoping for.

Three days later is Pharaoh's birthday, and we learn that Joseph's interpretation of both dreams are dead on—literally in the case of the baker who is beheaded. The cupbearer, on the other hand, is allowed to serve Pharaoh again. Unfortunately, after the cupbearer is restored to the king's service, he forgets about Joseph. Two years pass before Pharaoh begins to have troubling dreams of his own.

Pharaoh dreams of seven fine, fat cows grazing by the Nile River. Seven emaciated cows emerge from the Nile and devour the fat cows. The king wakes up troubled but goes back to sleep. Then, in the same night, he dreams of seven fat ears of grain growing on a stalk. Then seven pitifully thin ears grow and devour the healthy grain. Only after Pharaoh's troubling dreams begin does the cupbearer remember the Hebrew prisoner who had interpreted his dream. The cupbearer recommends Joseph to Pharaoh, and God gives Joseph the following interpretation: Seven years of great harvests will be followed by seven years of famine. That is the meaning of both dreams.

Pharaoh is baffled and terrified. Seven years of good yields will mean contentment among his people, but the seven years of famine will only bring discontent or even revolt and rebellion. What can he do? Fortunately, the Hebrew prisoner has a plan. Joseph tells Pharaoh to build storehouses and store grain during the seven years of feasting so there will be plenty of grain for Egyptians and even those beyond their borders during the seven years of famine.

The king likes Joseph's idea so well that he appoints the former slave and prisoner as head of the project. During the years of abundance, Joseph not only sets aside enough grain to save the world during the years of famine but also begins to favor Egyptian fashion, even taking an Egyptian name and an Egyptian wife. No one from Joseph's past life will recognize him as the bragging boy, the falsely accused slave, or the forgotten prisoner now.

Storytelling Prompts

1. Tell a story of a time when someone forgot a promise he or she made to you. The forgetting may have had small or large consequences for your life. How did being forgotten make you feel? In what ways were you aware of God's presence during this time?

2. Tell a story of a time when you forgot a promise you made to someone else. Did it have large or small consequences in his or her life? How did you learn about the result of your forgotten promise? What did you do when you found out? How did you try to fix the situation? How did your awareness of God's presence or lack of awareness shape your response?

Joseph's Spiritual Journey
Episode 4: Blessed to Be a Blessing

During the years of famine in Egypt, starving people from nearby countries begin to stream across the borders, hoping to purchase food. Among them are all of Joseph's brothers—the ones who had thrown him in the pit—except for his brother Benjamin. Their father has refused to allow the one he believes to be the only surviving son of his beloved Rachel to go with the others.

When the brothers arrive in Egypt, Joseph recognizes them, but they don't recognize him. This allows him to toy with them, accusing them of being spies and then placing them in a situation that he can require them to bring Benjamin, the brother they left behind, if they ever return. Joseph surmises that if he requires Benjamin to return with his brothers, then his father will come with them. Of course, Joseph's brothers must return to ask for more grain, and Joseph pulls a few additional tricks from his sleeve before he reveals to them who he really is—the brother they think they got rid of so many years ago.

As a child, Joseph, the dreamer, lived out a classic fantasy narrative as he shared his dreams of power, prestige, and grandeur with his brothers. His dreams most likely came from the favor his father showed him over his brothers, who naturally resented his "putting on airs" and resolved to get rid of both Joseph and his narcissistic fantasies. In doing so, they cast him both into a pit and into a life that had the potential to be shaped by a series of fear narratives.

The favored son with his grandiose dreams is left in a hole in the ground, captured by (or sold to) a caravan of people who are foreign to him, sold into slavery, accused of sexual assault, placed under arrest, and left to languish in confinement when someone he specifically asks to remember him forgets. I cannot begin to imagine a more fear-inducing series of events—especially for a young man who lived a pretty cushy life until his brothers took their revenge. At the close of the saga, Joseph toys with his brothers but resists taking revenge on them in turn. Joseph's story moves beyond fear and fantasy to conclude with him bringing his father, his brothers, and their families to Egypt. They settle in Goshen, where the land is fertile and can support growing crops and keeping animals. Joseph's story becomes one of faith.

The reason that the Joseph saga becomes a story of faith rather than merely a series of pleasant fantasies or frightening prospects can all be expressed in one phrase: *God was with him.* God's presence with Joseph is neither a form of wish fulfillment nor a shield of protection from the worst life can offer. While Joseph does become a wealthy, powerful, and influential official in Egypt, we are assured throughout his story that the aspect that characterizes his life narrative (dare we say spiritual journey) is the continuing presence of God. God is with Joseph when his life as his father's favorite child is wonderful, and God is with Joseph when he is in the hole in the ground, in slavery, and in prison.

Storytelling Prompts

1. Recall a time when you had an opportunity to do a good deed for someone who had either done you harm or not had your best interest at heart. Describe the circumstances, including the person who hurt you and how you felt. How did God's presence play a role in this experience?

2. Recall a time when someone did a good deed for you after you had done or wished him or her harm. Describe the circumstances, including the person who

performed the good deed and how you felt. How did God's presence play a role in this experience?

A Personal Story about the Biblical Story

Many years ago, one of my professors, Dr. Dorothy Jean (D. J.) Furnish, invited me to assist her with an intergenerational workshop titled "Experiencing the Bible with Children" at a large Presbyterian church in Florida. She had already been kind enough to ask me to write a chapter in her book of the same title on using storytelling to help children "meet with" the Bible. I was grateful to be asked to help her since she was a person for whom I held much respect. But I was also anxious since it was the first workshop of the kind I had helped to lead, and I wanted to do well.

D. J. and I were using a technique called story participation, for which two storytellers were required. We were leading a group of adults, teens, and children through the Joseph story that Saturday morning. I was the person telling the story, and D. J. was sitting with the listeners and joining them in portraying characters from the story. One reason for D. J.'s role—the person who sits and identifies with the listeners—is that if the listeners are required to move to another part of the room and one person (often a child) chooses not to go, the seated person can remain with the reluctant participant. This keeps the reluctant participant involved in the story without robbing him or her of the freedom to decline any request from the storyteller.

When I arrived at the point in the story when Joseph's brothers are sent by their father to ask the Egyptians for grain, one little girl refused to go. So I said, "That's okay because one brother, Benjamin, didn't go with the others. He stayed home with his father." (In this case, D. J. was playing the father.) Only after we had arrived in Egypt and were preparing to return home did I remember that Benjamin would have to accompany his brothers on the next trip or we would wind up rewriting the Bible substantially! At that moment, I felt the full force of my anxiety. I couldn't make the child come with us, nor would I have tried. What in the world would I do if she declined to come with us a second time?

As the participants and I prepared to make a second journey to Egypt to buy more grain, I wondered what would happen when it came time for Benjamin to join his brothers. When I reached that point in the story, I looked at the child, extended my hand, and said, "This time, Benjamin came with his brothers." The youngster looked up at me, smiled, took my hand, and off we went to Egypt. As I thought about that incident later, I realized that by allowing the girl the freedom to stay behind while also playing a part in the story, she had the opportunity to become one of the characters in her own way and in her own time. As Benjamin, she was willing to go with her brothers, even though she resisted the journey previously. I left with a hope that her fear and mine had become a story of faith and trust for both of us.

Before the workshop, I fantasized that everything would go without a hitch and I would be invited to do more of these types of workshops. But a narrative of fear also had me imagining that the workshop could go completely off the rails, leading my professor to regret asking me to lead in the first place. During the workshop, neither my fantasy nor my fear were fully realized. My moment of panic tapped into all my fears, but I faced them and learned to trust

the process, trust the child, and trust that God's presence
would lead me no matter the circumstances.

Jesus and Stories of Fear, Fantasy, and Faith

Jesus seems to have recognized the danger that stories of fear
and fantasy possess and how these stories can disrupt the
spiritual journey. He tells his followers again and again, "Do
not be afraid." (See Matthew 28:10; Mark 5:36, 6:50; Luke
12:4.) At the same time, he describes the fate he expects
when he arrives in Jerusalem—that he will be tried and cru-
cified. Neither the fears nor the fantasies of the disciples can
contain the reality of what God is about to do. Jesus knows
that the world holds many things that can frighten his followers. After all, the Jewish people are living under Roman
occupation, and they also deal with the commonplace dangers of sickness, accidents, violence, and death. Jesus is aware
of the dangers that surround him and his followers, but he
also realizes the power that fear has over people. Fear makes
people suspicious—even hateful—toward their neighbors,
especially if they are different from them. Fear can turn
them into the dangerous people whom others fear.

Jesus also recognizes the danger of a spiritual journey
based on creating fantasy worlds about the future. His
followers expect him to enter Jerusalem, overthrow the
Romans, reestablish a reign that replicates that of King
David, and appoint them all to high positions. Jesus warns
them about the risk of such expectations. Instead of living in an imperial fantasy world that offers him political
power and social privilege, he submits to a trial and the
worst form of execution that the Roman culture can come

up with (and the Romans are rather imaginative about torture and death).

Jesus does not give into the fear that anyone facing such a horrible death would naturally feel. Does that mean that Jesus is not afraid? Of course not. In the garden of Gethsemane, he prays that the bitter cup of flogging and crucifixion will pass by him so that he will not have to drink from it. Later, on the cross, he cries out, borrowing words from Psalm 22 and asking why God has forsaken him. Still, Jesus chooses not to live out of fear of Roman power and the pain that it inflicts, nor to live out of a fantasy grounded in attaining worldly power. He entrusts his story to God who allows him to live out a story of faith, defeating fear, fantasy, and even death.

A Jesus Story

In Luke 15:11-32, Jesus tells a story that presents the dangers of living out narratives of fantasy and fear and offers an example of the source for living a story of faith. This familiar story has many names, but I prefer to think of it as "The Son Who Went Away, the Father Who Waited, and the Son Who Stayed Home."

In the story, a father has two sons. The younger of the two lives in a fantasy of how great life would be if he could leave the farm with his share of his inheritance and live a life of the rich and famous. This fantasy presents a problem, however: He cannot receive his share of his father's estate until his father has died. To even ask his father for his inheritance would be an insult. But his dreams of the high life are too great, and he asks his father for his portion of the estate. Much to his amazement, his father says yes!

The younger son takes his share of the inheritance and lives out his fantasy narrative for a time. Jesus doesn't reveal the exact frivolities on which the son spent his money, but we as readers can guess. Inevitably, the young man's inheritance runs out. Living the life of the rich and famous means that when the riches go, the fame and money-hungry friends follow. These so-called friends disappear to find someone else who can afford to support the life to which they have become accustomed. The younger son must take a job to support himself, and the only one he can find involves feeding pigs. This is about the worst job a young Jewish man can take since swine are considered "unclean" in his faith tradition. He is so hungry that he is tempted to eat the slop that the pigs eat. He finds himself living out a story of fear that he never would have intentionally chosen. He fears for his life; he is afraid that he will starve.

Meanwhile, back at the farm, the older brother continues to work the fields and keep his father's flocks. He does so with great care because everything left will be his inheritance when his father dies. Perhaps he fantasizes about being the sole owner of his father's property now that his little brother is gone. Perhaps he also imagines what his younger sibling is doing with his part of the inheritance. His mind immediately goes to prostitutes, and he even mentions his suspicion later in the story.

The father simply waits and watches for his younger son to return, though he has no evidence to confirm or deny that his son will come home. Does he indulge in fantasies of his son's return? It's likely. Does he fear that his son may be gone forever? Almost surely, he does.

One day, the younger son comes to his senses. Instead of fearing starvation, he realizes he can return home and offer his services as a hired hand on his father's farm. After all, his father's tenants have a better life than he does. Stripped of his fantasies and fears, he heads home, trusting that his father will accept his apology and give him a job. He practices his apology all the way home.

The father sees his son coming in the distance. After all, he has been watching and waiting for this moment almost since the boy left. Throwing any semblance of dignity to the winds, the father hikes up his garment as if it were a long skirt and runs to meet his son. His neighbors may think he is crazy, but he can only focus on the fact that his son, whom he feared was dead, has returned alive. Once the father reaches his son, the son begins his practiced apology. The father stops him mid-sentence and calls for the calf he had been fattening up for a special occasion to be slaughtered. Then he calls for the robe, ring, and sandals that indicate that his son will not be hired on as a worker but will be welcomed back as a member of the family.

The party is going full blast by the time the older son finishes his work. When he asks a servant what is going on, the servant tells him that his younger brother has returned. The father invites the older brother to come into the party. The older son should have volunteered to help his father, but he is so deep in fear that his brother will get something of his that he can't even admit that they are related. "This son of yours . . . ," he says. "Wasting money on prostitutes . . . ," he says.

"This brother of yours," the father replies, "was dead and is now alive." And Jesus leaves the story hanging there. Will the older son respond to the father's invitation to release his fantasies and fears and love his brother? If so, how? Can we accept that invitation?

This story is one of faith. Beyond the fears of starvation, of losing a son, and of losing an inheritance is an image of a father, sitting, waiting, and watching. He is brooding—to borrow Hopkins's language—but without the negative connotations of the word. Every story of faith depends on steadfast love—on God's love—which we see embodied by the father. This love is extended by a waiting father to a son who may never return; it is extended to a son who resists celebrating his brother's return. And it is extended to us as well.

Jesus' story reminds us that beyond stories of fear and fantasy resides God's steadfast love, which never ends or fails. We can trust in God's presence as a force for good and healing through the best and worst of circumstances. This is "God's grandeur." By trusting in God's love, we move through stories of fear and fantasy and discover a deeper trust that doesn't depend on the circumstances of our lives but on God's faithfulness.

Storytelling Prompts

1. Tell a story of a time when you hurt someone and then had to go to him or her for help. How did you feel? How did that person respond?
2. Recall a time when you felt that someone else was getting favorable treatment and you were not. How did you react? What did you do?
3. Tell a story of a time when you felt unsure of God's love. If this was a difficult time in your life, describe the circumstances and how God felt absent from your life. What did you do to remind yourself of God's abiding presence?

CONCLUSION

While our earthly lives end in death, stories about our days on this earth have an afterlife. As a pastor for more than forty years, I have had the privilege of sitting with numerous families after they experienced the death of a loved one. As we plan a service to celebrate the life and faith of a deceased family member, those who love him or her quite naturally begin to share stories. "Do you remember the time that she . . . ?" "I will never forget when he. . . ." "She always did. . . ." "He always said. . . ." The sharing might begin with a question from me or a story from another family member, but soon one remembrance leads to another. Before long, the atmosphere is thick with the presence of that person. Though he or she may not be physically present with us, he or she is with us in memory and in story. If I don't know the deceased person, I am almost completely dependent on those family stories to get a sense of the way the person's life reflected his or her faith. Often, after hearing moving stories and funny anecdotes, I wind up wishing I had known that person better.

When I was appointed to West End United Methodist Church in Nashville, Tennessee, I began visiting church member and retired United Methodist bishop Roy Clark. I first met Roy Clark when I became a member of the

Tennessee Conference in 1974. At that time, he was serving as senior pastor at West End UMC. Though visiting
him fell under the category of pastoral responsibility, I also
considered our time together to be one of inspiration and
mentorship as he shared his experience and wisdom with
me. I knew that Roy had been a leader in the integration of
churches in his home conference in Mississippi and that he
had served in Memphis before pastoring at West End. In
one of our conversations, he shared a story from the early
days of his ministry that demonstrated the importance
of knowing the stories of our congregants as we prepare
funerals or memorial services.

As a young pastor serving a small church in rural
Mississippi, Roy found himself in an odd predicament. A
moonshiner in the community died, and though he was
not a member of the church Roy served, the young pastor
was expected to conduct the funeral service. The deceased
moonshiner had two different families who still lived in the
community, so Roy went to one family to ask for stories
about him. The family told him that they didn't want to
share any stories for fear that they would offend the other
family. So the dutiful young preacher trekked to the other
family to make a similar request. Their answer was the
same as the first family. They were afraid to share stories
lest they offend the other family. Roy was left to prepare a
eulogy for a man he did not know and about whom he had
collected no stories. After the service, one of his church
members approached him and said, "Preacher, that was the
worst funeral I ever heard preached. Why, I couldn't tell if
you were burying a man or a horse!"

The sad truth is that without others continuing to tell
our stories after we are gone from this earth, we might as
well be a horse. The people who have formed and shaped

our lives while they were among us can still live inside us and influence the way we live even after their death. In some sense, as long as we continue to tell the stories of loved ones, they remain a presence within us and among us.

As Christians, we retell the same essential stories throughout the church year—stories of our many ancestors in faith and, most importantly, the stories told by and about Jesus. At funerals and memorial services, we tell stories of those persons whose memory will continue to grow in and enrich our lives. On All Saints' Day, we tell stories of those witnesses who have gone before us. Their stories provide examples of moving beyond fear and fantasy to build a life of faith. The places, people, and circumstances of their lives will continue to help us weave the presence of the Holy into our own lives. The narratives of their divine encounters prepare us to open our lives to God's grandeur and to recognize our own divine encounters.

The lives of storytellers may come to an end, but stories continue. In a hundred years, no one will remember the name *Michael E. Williams*, but the stories of scripture—narratives of fear, fantasy, and faith—will continue to be told. Just as my Aintie passed on stories to me, I pass them on to my children, to those in the congregations I have served, and to you. Now it is up to you to pass them on to others, who will pass them on to others, who will . . . well, you know. Let's keep the stories going.

ABOUT THE AUTHOR

Michael E. Williams is a United Methodist pastor who served in the Tennessee Conference for over forty years, most recently as senior pastor at West End United Methodist Church in Nashville. The author of numerous articles, stories, poems, plays, and books, he was general editor of The Storyteller's Companion to the Bible series (Abingdon Press). Michael has been a featured storyteller at the National Storytelling Festival. He and his wife, Margaret, live in Nashville and have two adult daughters. Presently, he is Poet/Storyteller-in-Residence at Martin Methodist College in Pulaski, Tennessee.

For those who hunger for deep spiritual experience . . .

The Academy for Spiritual Formation® is an experience of disciplined Christian community emphasizing holistic spirituality—nurturing body, mind, and spirit. The program, a ministry of The Upper Room®, is ecumenical in nature and meant for all those who hunger for a deeper relationship with God, including both lay and clergy. Each Academy fosters spiritual rhythms—of study and prayer, silence and liturgy, solitude and relationship, rest and exercise. With offerings of both Two-Year and Five-Day models, Academy participants rediscover Christianity's rich spiritual heritage through worship, learning, and fellowship. The Academy's commitment to an authentic spirituality promotes balance, inner and outer peace, holy living and justice living—God's shalom.

Faculty trained in the wide breadth of Christian spirituality and practice provide content and guidance at each session of The Academy. Academy faculty presenters come from seminaries, monasteries, spiritual direction ministries, and pastoral ministries or other settings and are from a variety of traditions. Frank Rogers is on the list of faculty for The Academy and currently serves on The Academy Advisory Board.

The ACADEMY RECOMMENDS program seeks to highlight content that aligns with the Academy's mission to provide resources and settings where pilgrims encounter the teachings, sustaining practices, and rhythms that foster attentiveness to God's Spirit and therefore help spiritual leaders embody Christ's presence in the world.

Learn more here: http://academy.upperroom.org/.